What *Did* Jesus Do?

What *Did* Jesus Do?

The Biblical Roots
of the Catholic Church

Thomas J. Nash

Incarnate Word Media
Ann Arbor, Michigan

Published by Incarnate Word Media
Distributed by Thomson-Shore
7300 West Joy Road
Dexter, MI 48130
https://thomsonshore.com/

Printed With Ecclesiastical Permission.
Most Reverend Earl Boyea. May 16, 2017.

Cover design by Riz Boncan Marsella

Cover art: "Christ Giving the Keys of the Kingdom to St. Peter"
(detail), Pietro Perugino, Sistine Chapel, Vatican City.

Cover photograph copyright © www.gettyimages.com
St. Peter's Basilica and Square at dusk, Vatican City.

To Mike, Chris, Rose, Tim, Tricia and Dave,
In gratitude for your steadfast love in challenging times.
May we all one day together, please Lord,
join Mom, Dad, Mary, Catherine
and our three miscarried siblings
whose names we know not yet in
that wondrous heavenly reunion.

(see Jn. 11:25–26)

Peter and the apostles answered,
"We must obey God rather than men. . . .

When they heard this they were enraged
and wanted to kill them.
But a Pharisee in the council named Gamali-el,
a teacher of the law, held in honor by all the people,
stood up and ordered the men to be put outside for a while.
And he said to them, "Men of Israel, take care
what you do with these men.
For before these days Theudas arose,
giving himself out to be somebody,
and a number of men, about four hundred,
joined him; but he was slain and all who
followed him were dispersed and came to nothing.
After him Judas the Galilean arose in the days of
the census and drew away some of the people after him;
he also perished, and all who followed him were scattered.
So in the present case I tell you, keep away from these men
and let them alone; for if this plan or this undertaking
is of men, it will fail; but if it is of God,
you will not be able to overthrow them.
You might even be found opposing God!"

(Acts 5:29, 33–39)

Contents

Abbreviations and Acronyms 9

Foreword by Al Kresta 11

Preface
"Who Cares What Jesus Did?"
The Perennial Relevance of Christ and His Church 13

Introduction
Anything We Can Do, God Can Do Better
Building a Church to Last 27

1. **"He Who Hears You Hears Me"**
God's Use of Human Leaders
throughout Salvation History 41

2. **Knowing God's Saving Word**
The Bible Alone?
Or Scripture, Tradition and the Magisterium? 57

3. **"What Must I Do to Be Saved?"**
Successfully Navigating the Highway to Heaven 77

4. **"Do This in Memory of Me"**
The Fundamental Importance of
the Sacrifice of the Eucharist (Mass)/Lord's Supper . . . 107

5. **How Many Airborne Divisions**
Does the Church Militant Got?
A Celestial Army of Angels and Saints 139

6. **"Be Perfect, as Your Heavenly Father Is Perfect"**
Drawing Closer to Christ and Preparing for Heaven
by Celebrating and Living the Sacraments 153

7. **"To Whom Shall We Go?"**
Jesus has Given His Catholic Church
the Words and Mission of Eternal Life 179

Appendix 207

Scripture Index 217

Catechism of the Catholic Church (CCC) Index 225

Abbreviations and Acronyms

THE OLD TESTAMENT

Gen	Genesis
Ex	Exodus
Lev	Leviticus
Num	Numbers
Deut	Deuteronomy
Josh	Joshua
Judg	Judges
Ruth	Ruth
1 Sam	1 Samuel
2 Sam	2 Samuel
1 Kings	1 Kings
2 Kings	2 Kings
1 Chron	1 Chronicles
2 Chron	2 Chronicles
Ezra	Ezra
Neh	Nehemiah
Tob	Tobit
Jud	Judith
Esther	Esther
Job	Job
Ps	Psalms
Prov	Proverbs
Eccles	Ecclesiastes
Song	Song of Solomon
Wis	Wisdom
Sir	Sirach (Ecclesiasticus)
Is	Isaiah
Jer	Jeremiah
Lam	Lamentations
Bar	Baruch
Ezek	Ezekiel
Dan	Daniel
Hos	Hosea
Joel	Joel
Amos	Amos
Obad	Obadiah
Jon	Jonah
Mic	Micah
Nahum	Nahum
Hab	Habakkuk
Zeph	Zephaniah
Hag	Haggai
Zech	Zechariah
Mal	Malachi
1 Mac	1 Maccabees
2 Mac	2 Maccabees

THE NEW TESTAMENT

Mt	Matthew
Mk	Mark
Lk	Luke
Jn	John
Acts	Acts of the Apostles
Rom	Romans
1 Cor	1 Corinthians
2 Cor	2 Corinthians
Gal	Galatians
Eph	Ephesians
Phil	Philippians
Col	Colossians
1 Thess	1 Thessalonians
2 Thess	2 Thessalonians
1 Tim	1 Timothy
2 Tim	2 Timothy
Tit	Titus
Philem	Philemon
Heb	Hebrews
Jas	James
1 Pet	1 Peter
2 Pet	2 Peter
1 Jn	1 John
2 Jn	2 John
3 Jn	3 John
Jude	Jude
Rev	Revelation (Apocalypse)

CCC   *Catechism of the Catholic Church*

Foreword

What Western Christians call "denominationalism" didn't exist before the so-called Reformation of 1517. By 1600, however, the various reform movements had deteriorated into a cacophony of competing confessions (denominations), sustained and enforced by the power of states which rivaled one another and often longed to usurp the prerogatives of the Papacy.

Tom Nash knows that this creedal competition was not Jesus' will for his Church. He works hard to avoid demonizing polemics and labors to settle the argument by appealing to our Protestant brothers and sisters on our common ground of Scripture. He is confident that Jesus can settle the argument.

To that end, he asks what kind of Church did Jesus intend to build? What materials were used to construct it? How does he currently govern it? This rich encounter with the Church of the Scriptures results in "Aha" after "Aha" moment. Nash demonstrates that Jesus didn't perform a bait and switch, promising a kingdom and then delivering a cheapened, fraudulent facsimile called "the church." The Church wasn't an afterthought, a mere pragmatic association of Jesus people. Rather, Jesus, from the beginning, willed the Church to be the center of human history and the Eucharistic Sacrifice to be the center of ecclesial identity and worship.

11

Nash's arguments are carefully constructed, well-organized and delivered in fresh, lively prose that trusts the Church's founder to mean what he says. Catholics will be reinforced in their faith and stretched in their spiritual imaginations. They may have never considered such a grand vision of the Church. But non-Catholics will also be grateful for this engagement of Scripture that clears up misconceptions and can only lead to more honest and fruitful relations between Catholics and the "separated brethren." Buy it, read it, share it during this five-hundredth year since the unity of Western Christendom[1] was ruptured and sizeable communities of Christians hardened into denominations. You never know what you might contribute to reunion.

— Al Kresta

President and CEO of Ave Maria Radio and Host of the internationally syndicated talk-radio program "Kresta in the Afternoon"

---

[1] "The unity of Western Christendom" here refers to once-Catholic Europe, not the divine mark of unity which the Church can never lose (see CCC 811–16).

Preface

"Who Cares What Jesus Did?"

The Perennial Relevance of Christ and His Church

Given widespread skepticism in modern times, many may read the title of this book and simply reply, "Who really cares?" And move on.

For many, Jesus Christ is a good moral teacher, but only one of a good number in history. For others, Jesus is a polarizing figure, based on their faith heritage and/or other experiences they and their loved ones, including perhaps their ancestors, have had with Christians. For still others, given that they doubt God's existence or resolutely don't believe, Jesus is not seen as a consequential figure in their everyday lives. And for people in each of these three groups, Jesus' "hard sayings" (Jn. 6:60) and the reform those teachings would require in their lives also make him a polarizing figure.

In any of these variations, Jesus would not be recognized as Almighty God in the flesh, one who came to die for their sins and reconcile them to himself.[1] Or if they were inclined to recognize his divinity, Christ's moral demands would be seen as a deterrent to their assent. And there are many others—i.e., non-Catholic Christians of various

---

[1] There are even those who will question whether Jesus existed, but their numbers are relatively few and there are no credible scholars among them.

backgrounds—who would agree on the relevance of Jesus but *not* the relevance of the Catholic Church.

But is Jesus who he said he is?

In his bestselling book *Mere Christianity*, Anglican author C. S. Lewis argues that Jesus could not truly be a good moral teacher unless he was also God. To argue to the contrary, Lewis says, would be "really foolish,"[2] when one considers the evidence of the four Gospels. After all, Jesus claims that he can forgive sins—any sins—that he has always existed, and that he will come to judge the world at the end of time. Such a man could only be the Lord God, a liar or a lunatic, as Lewis' trilemma has come to be known. He could not simply be "a great moral teacher."[3]

Think about it. Jesus cannot be admired as a great moral teacher, all the while being a "deceiver" or a "nutjob." We're talking here about an oil-and-water mixture that doesn't go together. That *can't* go together. It is because Jesus does things that only God can do, and says things about himself that can only be understood as claims to divinity, that simply characterizing the Lord as a "great moral teacher" is ruled out.

As Lewis notes well, the four Gospels do not present a Jesus who is mentally unhinged, but rather one who is wonderfully human, speaking with wisdom and authority that command the attention of the religious authorities of his day. He also exemplifies merciful love to those in most need, such as the woman caught in adultery who was about

---

[2] C. S. Lewis, *Mere Christianity*, rev. and enlarg. ed. (New York: Collier Books; Macmillan Publishing Company, 1952), 55.

[3] Ibid., 56.

to be stoned, or various others who suffered from serious illness or demonic possession.

Lewis uses the words "Lord" and "lunatic," a madman with deep delusions, but he actually opts for a much harsher term than "liar," namely, "the Devil of Hell." For he says only a demon would be worthy of such a profound falsehood.[4] But Jesus is not a liar. When questioned whether he has the authority to forgive sins, Jesus doesn't cut and run, a discovered fraud. He visibly demonstrates that authority by healing a paralytic (Mt. 9:2–8). And when Jesus says he will die but rise from the dead, he follows through with his glorious Resurrection, as the four Gospels attest.

Jesus also *rebukes and exorcises* demons; he *isn't one himself*. Demons may tell the truth, but only in the temporary service of their deceptive plans—"to steal and kill and destroy," as Jesus says (Jn. 10:10). In marked contrast, Jesus allows himself to be destroyed, to be killed for our sins, so that we "may have life, and have it abundantly" (Jn. 10:10).

Demons don't get taken down by mere human forces. But if God became man, it's conceivable that he might willingly die in the interest of saving the whole world (see Jn. 3:16–17; Mt. 16:21; Lk. 22:37).

Lord, Liar, Lunatic . . . or Legend?

Given modern skepticism about the Gospels' reliability as witnesses to the sayings and doings of Jesus, however,

---

[4] Ibid.

Fr. Ronald Tacelli and Dr. Peter Kreeft consider a fourth option for Jesus' identity: "myth," i.e., a legend. In other words, these two philosophers say, "Suppose the liar is not Jesus but the New Testament texts."[5] They argue that "if a mythic 'layer' had been added onto an originally merely human Jesus, we should find at least _some_ evidence, at least indirectly and secondhand, of this earlier layer. We find instead an absolute and total absence of any such evidence anywhere, either internal (in the New Testament texts themselves) or external, anywhere else, in Christian, anti-Christian, or non-Christian sources."[6] One would expect contemporary non-Christian sources—particularly Christian opponents like the leaders of the reigning Roman Empire—to set the record straight on Jesus' identity, especially if it served their purposes. But there is no such evidence.

And in comparison with other ancient written works, we have at least 10 times more copies of the New Testament.[7] Why is that significant? Well, the more copies of a written work you have—in this case the manuscripts of the New Testament writings—the better able you are to establish what the original wording is. This is a fundamental part of what is known as "textual criticism." In this case, the goal is to hopefully impart confidence that the story of Jesus is reliable in its _telling_ (historicity of the Gospels) as well

---

[5] Peter Kreeft and Ronald K. Tacelli, _Handbook of Christian Apologetics: Hundreds of Answers to Crucial Questions_ (Downers Grove, IL: InterVarsity Press, 1994), 161.

[6] Ibid., 163.

[7] Ibid., 162. For example, there are 500 copies of the New Testament that date earlier than A.D. 500, whereas there are only 50 copies of the _Iliad_ within 500 years of when Homer wrote it in the ninth century B.C.

as in its *transmission* (integrity of the Gospels). In other words, do they reliably record what Jesus did, and is there consistency between the respective copies of the Gospels and other New Testament books?

Kreeft and Tacelli report that the New Testament stands up well to textual analysis, noting that the discrepancies between the manuscripts are "very few" and that there are "*no* really important ones." "And all later discoveries of manuscripts, such as the Dead Sea Scrolls," they add, "have confirmed rather than refuted previously existing manuscripts in every important case. There is simply no other ancient text in nearly as good a shape."[8]

In his book *The Case for Jesus: The Biblical and Historical Evidence for Christ*, Dr. Brant Pitre, a Scripture scholar, also addresses claims that the Jesus of the Gospels is a legendary figure. Modern critics, he says, argue that later, anonymous storytellers wrote the four Gospels based on faulty oral tradition, instead of the firsthand testimony of eyewitnesses (St. Matthew and St. John) or non-eyewitnesses who relied on the reports of eyewitnesses (St. Mark and St. Luke).[9] The four Gospels circulated anonymously for about 100 years, so the theory goes, and then the names of the four evangelists were added to the opening page of each Gospel to boost their credibility.[10]

---

[8] Ibid., emphasis original.

[9] Brant Pitre, *The Case for Jesus: The Biblical and Historical Evidence for Christ* (New York: Image, 2016), 26–38. Pitre says that John may have dictated his Gospel, though he may have written it as well (36–38). In either case, he would have been the author of its contents.

[10] Ibid., 12–15.

In fact, Pitre says, no anonymous Gospel manuscripts exist, and he provides a list of both complete and fragmentary manuscripts that date from the second to the fifth centuries; each one is ascribed to one of the four evangelists.[11] And if the Gospels circulated widely throughout various countries *before* being falsely given names, you'd expect a variety of persons named as authors for the manuscripts in general, as well as contradictions regarding who authored certain manuscripts in particular, especially given that there are four different Gospel accounts. But there are no such variations and contradictions regarding authorship of the Gospel manuscripts, and there is no evidence otherwise claiming that the evangelists' names were later added.[12] Only the four evangelists are named as authors.

Furthermore, if credibility were a real concern, why not attribute a Gospel to one of the 11 bona fide apostles who walked with Jesus, particularly prominent ones like St. Peter and St. James, who worked closely with the Lord? Or perhaps St. Paul, the subsequent apostolic luminary? Attributing a Gospel to non-eyewitnesses such as Mark and Luke seems rather improbable, unless . . . they actually were the authors of their respective Gospels.[13] And why St. Matthew, who was not a prominent apostle? "Even more," says Curtis Mitch, the annotator of *The Ignatius Catholic Study Bible New Testament*, "it is unlikely that a Gospel addressed to readers from a Jewish background would be attributed to

---

[11] Ibid., 15–18.

[12] Ibid., 18–20.

[13] See Curtis Mitch's essay "Introduction to the Gospels" in *The Ignatius Catholic Study Bible New Testament* (San Francisco: Ignatius Press, 2010), xv–xxiii.

a tax collector, since tax collectors were generally despised by Jews as morally corrupt, ritually unclean and politically traitorous." Unless, ironically enough, Matthew is the actual author.[14]

Quite unlike the four Gospels, Pitre says, the New Testament Letter to the Hebrews[15] "is *actually anonymous*. It never explicitly identifies its author, not even in the title. So guess what happens when you have a real anonymous book? It ends up either remaining anonymous or being attributed to different authors,"[16] as Pitre shows in a chart of manuscripts from the second to the eleventh centuries, with the earlier ones listing no author and later ones ascribing authorship to St. Paul or his confrere St. Timothy:

> That's what you get with a truly anonymous book of the New Testament: actual anonymous manuscripts, and actual ancient debates over who wrote it. But that's precisely what you *don't* find when it comes to the Gospels of Matthew, Mark, Luke and John. No anonymous copies, and . . . no debate among ancient Christians over who wrote the Gospels. Scholars who continue to claim the Gospels were originally anonymous cannot explain why we don't find the same variety of suggested authors as we do with the Letter to the Hebrews.[17]

---

[14] Ibid., xvi.

[15] Scholars date the Letter to the Hebrews from the 60s to the 80s (A.D.). See *The Ignatius Catholic Study Bible New Testament*, 413.

[16] Pitre, *The Case for Jesus*, 20, emphasis original.

[17] Ibid., 22. Other suggested authors include St. Barnabas, St. Paul's companion, and St. Clement of Rome, the fourth Pope.

St. John's Gospel was the last written, perhaps as late as A.D. 100.[18] John presents some of Jesus' strongest claims to divinity, including John 8:57–59, 14:6–9 and 17:20–23. Many modern scholars doubt the historicity of these claims, though, because they say Jesus does not claim to be God in the respective synoptic Gospels[19] of Sts. Matthew, Mark and Luke.[20] And if three out of four Gospels don't affirm Jesus' divinity, they add, the other one must be inaccurate.

Pitre says these scholars miss the distinctively Jewish way that Jesus proclaims his divinity, specifically in how he performs certain miracles, e.g., his stilling of a storm and walking on water. While mere human beings may be empowered by God to perform miracles, in the Old Testament only God calms the sea and saves those in distress (Psalm 107). Jesus does the same with his disciples, as recorded in Matthew 8, Mark 4 and Luke 8.[21] Similarly, in Matthew 14, Mark 6 and John 6, Jesus walks on water, reassuring his disciples by simply identifying himself as "I am" (_egō eimi_ in the Greek language of these Gospels).[22] "I am"—"Yahweh" or "YHWH" in Hebrew—is the name God uses to identify himself to Moses (Ex. 3:14), when he calls the great prophet to lead his people out of Egyptian bondage. "I am" conveys that God's essence is existence. That is,

---

[18] _The Ignatius Catholic Study Bible New Testament_, 157.

[19] The synoptic Gospels are so named because they take a similar view in presenting the life of Jesus.

[20] Pitre, _The Case for Jesus_, 7, 120–21.

[21] Ibid., 122–26.

[22] Ibid., 126–31.

his nature is simply to exist. He has no beginning or end, which is only true of one who is eternal.

That's why some Jews picked up stones to kill Jesus in John 8; because in saying "before Abraham was, I am," Jesus takes for himself the divine name of Yahweh, claiming oneness with the God of Israel, which to many of his Jewish listeners constituted blasphemy. There are other examples that affirm Jesus' divinity, including his claim to forgive anyone's sins and then backing it up by healing a paralytic (Mt. 9:2–8). A similar claim to divinity deemed blasphemous by Jewish leaders sealed Jesus' death (Mt. 26:63–68).

In summary, the Gospels can withstand various criticism that their portrayal of Jesus is simply legendary, and yet their central claim—that Jesus *is* God—is one that cannot be proven by the texts themselves, and so is one for which skeptics understandably desire more evidence.

Jesus and "The Sign of Jonah"

Pitre provides a keen insight from the Gospels to help resolve the matter. When the scribes and Pharisees ask Jesus for a sign to establish his legitimacy, Jesus tells them that no sign shall be given to them except the sign of Jonah (Mt. 12:38–40). Pitre argues that a close reading of Jonah 1:17—3:3 reveals that Jonah actually died in the whale and was brought back to life, a rising that anticipated Jesus' Resurrection.[23]

---

[23] Pitre, 185–88.

Yet, as the popular TV pitch promotes, "But wait! There's more!" An integral part of the sign of Jonah is the remarkable repentance—at least for a time—of the _Gentile_ city of Nineveh. And not just any city, but the capital of Assyria, one of Israel's most formidable pagan enemies. So when Jesus says he will provide the sign of Jonah as a reason to believe in him, he's not simply pointing to his Resurrection from the dead, but proclaiming that many Gentiles would come to believe in him.[24]

In fact, Jesus' goal was much more daunting than Jonah's. Jonah got a whole city to repent, whereas Jesus tells his apostles to make disciples of _all_ "nations," i.e., the "Gentiles" (Mt. 28:18–20), which, if accomplished, would be a universal or "catholic" sign. To accomplish this remarkable goal, Jesus builds his Church on St. Peter, the first Pope, who alone had "the keys of the kingdom of heaven" in leading the Church with his brother apostles (Mt. 16: 18–19).

Has the Sign Been Fulfilled?

What has happened since Jesus spoke those words about Jonah and himself 2,000 years ago? The early Church Fathers provide a stunning report. For example, writing in the late fourth century St. Ambrose, Bishop of Milan, says, "The mystery of the Church is clearly expressed. Her flocks stretch from the boundaries of the whole world. They

---

[24] Ibid., 188–91

stretch to Nineveh through penitence. . . . The mystery is now fulfilled in truth."[25]

But perhaps the most eloquent testimony regarding the fulfillment of Jesus' sign of Jonah comes from a non-Catholic historian from Great Britain, Thomas Babington Macaulay.[26] Writing in 1840 in the *Edinburgh Review*, Macaulay chronicles the remarkable success and endurance of the Catholic Church:

> There is not, and there never was on this earth, a work of human policy so well deserving of examination as the Roman Catholic Church. The history of that Church joins together the two great ages of human civilisation. No other institution is left standing which carries the mind back to the times when the smoke of sacrifice rose from the Pantheon, and when camelopards[27] and tigers bounded in the Flavian amphitheatre.
>
> The proudest royal houses are but of yesterday, when compared with the line of the Supreme Pontiffs. That line we trace back in an unbroken series, from the Pope who crowned Napoleon in the nineteenth century to the Pope who crowned Pepin in the eighth; and far beyond the time of Pepin the august dynasty extends, till it is lost in the twilight of fable.
>
> The republic of Venice came next in antiquity. But the republic of Venice was modern when compared with the Papacy; and the republic of Venice is gone, and the Papacy remains. The Papacy remains, not in decay, not a mere antique, but full of life and youthful vigour.

---

[25] St. Ambrose, *Exposition of the Gospel of Luke*, 7.96. As cited in Arthur Just, Jr., *Ancient Christian Commentary on Scripture: New Testament III, Luke*, 3rd ed. (Downers Grove, IL: IVP Academic, 2003), 196.

[26] https://www.britannica.com/biography/Thomas-Babington-Macaulay-Baron-Macaulay.

[27] An archaic name for giraffes.

What _Did_ Jesus Do?

The Catholic Church is still sending forth to the farthest ends of the world missionaries as zealous as those who landed in Kent with Augustin, and still confronting hostile kings with the same spirit with which she confronted Attila. The number of her children is greater than in any former age. Her acquisitions in the New World have more than compensated for what she has lost in the Old. Her spiritual ascendency extends over the vast countries which lie between the plains of the Missouri and Cape Horn, countries which a century hence, may not improbably contain a population as large as that which now inhabits Europe. The members of her communion are certainly not fewer than a hundred and fifty million; and it will be difficult to show that all other Christian sects united amount to a hundred and twenty million.

Nor do we see any sign which indicates that the term of her long dominion is approaching. She saw the commencement of all the governments and of all the ecclesiastical establishments that now exist in the world; and we feel no assurance that she is not destined to see the end of them all. She was great and respected before the Saxon had set foot on Britain, before the Frank had passed the Rhine, when Grecian eloquence still flourished at Antioch, when idols were still worshipped in the temple of Mecca. And she may still exist in undiminished vigour when some traveller from New Zealand shall, in the midst of a vast solitude, take his stand on a broken arch of London Bridge to sketch the ruins of St. Paul's.[28]

And almost 2,000 years after the Resurrection, during which time we've seen many signs and wonders attesting to the credibility of Catholicism (CCC 156), the Church remains as relevant as ever—precisely because the God-man

---

[28] http://www.victorianweb.org/authors/macaulay/ranke1.html.

Jesus Christ is her founder and spiritual guarantor. With more than a billion believers and an impact that is indeed worldwide, the Church continues her God-given mission. If the Church were merely a human institution, she would not have survived centuries of persecution and also self-inflicted wounds by her members.

If God did not become man, i.e., "if the Incarnation did not really happen, then an even more unbelievable miracle happened," say Kreeft and Tacelli, paraphrasing St. Thomas Aquinas. That miracle is "the conversion of the world by the biggest lie in history and the moral transformation of lives into unselfishness, detachment from worldly pleasures and radically new heights of holiness by a mere myth."[29]

As St. Ambrose, Macaulay and a host of others can attest, God *did* become man and he has empowered his Church to do remarkable and miraculous things over the centuries. Why did Jesus found the Catholic Church? How did Jesus establish his Church? We'll address these issues further in the Introduction, and then in various ways throughout the book. In the process, we'll address the major figures of the Protestant Reformation[30] and their respective key

---

[29] Kreeft and Tacelli, *Handbook of Christian Apologetics*, 157. In his *Summa Contra Gentiles*, St. Thomas says, "It would be more wonderful than all other miracles, if without miraculous signs the world had been induced by simple and low-born men to believe truths so arduous, to do works so difficult, to hope for reward so high"; bk. 1, ch. 6, sect. 1; http://www3.nd.edu/Departments/Maritain/etext/gc1_6.htm. Here Thomas refers to practical or moral truths that are hard to live and thus are arduous, particularly if God doesn't exist and we therefore don't have his grace to help us live them.

[30] The terms "Protestant Reformation" and "Reformers" are used because they are familiar to many people, and these words also avoid needless polemics associated with terms like "Protestant Revolt." Yet, I will endeavor to make

doctrines, which have served and continue to serve as counterclaims to "What _Did_ Jesus Do?" And I'll strive to offer hope for an epic reunion between Catholics and Protestants, as well as for advancing the mission to make disciples of all nations otherwise. It can only happen in and through Jesus Christ.

---

clear in this book that any hope the Reformers had for true reform ended, when they rejected the divinely given authority of the Pope and began to establish other doctrinal novelties.

In addition, the Church was undoubtedly in need of reform at the time of the Reformation, albeit not in terms of doctrine but regarding certain actions of some of her human leaders. For an excellent overview in this regard, see Karl Adam, _The Roots of the Reformation_ (New York: Sheed and Ward, 1951), 7–29.

Introduction

Anything We Can Do, God Can Do Better

Building a Church to Last

Imagine that the United States had nothing but its Constitution, with no clearly established government, i.e., a living institution set up to implement, interpret and enforce the provisions of this famous political compact. Whatever you think of past and present U.S. Presidents (Executive Branch), Congresses (Legislative Branch) and Supreme Court justices (Judicial Branch),[1] imagine what living in America would be like if those governmental structures never existed.

Or, imagine if those three governing branches suddenly ceased to exist. And the respective state and local governments with them. What would living in the United States be like?

Can you imagine the political unrest? The social disarray? The anarchy that would ensue in the absence of an established governmental authority to make, carry out and evaluate our laws?

"What's your point?" you may well be thinking. "The Founding Fathers, supported by a fledgling citizenry, were

---

[1] https://www.usa.gov/branches-of-government.

smart enough to avoid anarchy, enshrining a unique form of government in adopting the U.S. Constitution. You can't advance a country's mission—whether in the United States or elsewhere—without some type of recognized and safeguarded form of government."

Well, that's *precisely* my point.

If mere human beings are wise enough to form governments to establish and sustain the mission of their countries—governments whose authority extends only to temporal or earthly affairs—how much more should we expect from God, whose mission[2] is the eternal salvation of all mankind?

Flawed from the Beginning:
Reforming Christianity apart from God's Church

If you believe in God, or at least can posit God's existence for the sake of argument, you'd expect God's intelligence to surpass that of mere human persons whom he created in his image and likeness (see Gen. 1:26–27). He who is omniscient would have to be able to come up with a better plan, and he who is omnipotent would have to have the power to carry that plan to fruition.

In making such a reasoned reflection, we can see—charitably stated—the fundamental flaw of the Protestant

---

[2] One might argue that "mission" implies "sending," and that no one sends God. However, we're not speaking of mere human forces' commissioning Jesus. Rather, the Father sent his eternal Son to save the world (Jn. 3:16) and the Son obediently conformed. So the word "mission" is appropriate in this context.

Reformation,[3] namely, jettisoning the divinely ordained teaching and governing authority Jesus Christ provided in establishing his Church, i.e., the Catholic Church. This rejection of Church authority dramatically undermined the cause of Christian unity,[4] and has resulted in the formation of tens of thousands of denominations over the past 500 years.[5]

---

[3] On the use of terms like "Protestant Reformation" and "Reformers," see footnote 30 of the Preface.

[4] The Church's mark of unity is a divinely given quality she can never lose, but the Church can *add or subtract members*. Subtraction effectively occurs when someone formally or informally repudiates their Catholic faith for one reason or another. The Church is also hurt by tepid members, including those Catholics who are registered in parishes but don't participate in Sunday Mass regularly.

[5] The *World Christian Encyclopedia* (WCE) says that, as of mid-2000, the number of Christian denominations was more than 33,000; http://www.worldchristi andatabase.org/wcd/. However, the WCE's calculation methods have received criticism, e.g., that Catholics in communion with the Pope should be treated as one entity, not listed as 242 different groups because of geographical and complementary worship differences, and that many in the "Marginals" category (1,600 in total) should not be listed at all, including the Mormons and Jehovah's Witnesses, because they don't affirm the Christian fundamentals of Jesus' divinity and the reality of the Trinity. See Scott Eric Alt's "We Need to Stop Saying That There Are 33,000 Protestant Denominations," *National Catholic Register*, February 9, 2016; http://www.ncregister.com/blog/scottericalt/we-need-to-stop-saying-that-there-are-33000-protestant-denominations.

On the other hand, the WCE and its defenders will say that many Christian denominations are rightly counted separately, because even though they may share common doctrine, they have independent governmental oversight, thereby showing an aversion to the greater unity and mutually recognized authority one should expect from a group of Christians calling themselves unified, and that even if listed in the "Independent" category vs. "Protestant," they ultimately derive their roots from the Reformation and

This is certainly not to say that the Catholic Church has never been in need of reform, whether regarding the witness of the Church's clerical leadership, consecrated men and women religious, or lay people in general. Rather, I'm simply saying that any reforms need to respect the authoritative structures and teachings that Jesus has provided for his Church.

Throughout salvation history, God has always worked to lead his people through human leaders he commissioned. In Old Testament times, those leaders included Abraham, Moses and King David. Each of those men had their flaws, yet God did not remove them from leading his people because of their transgressions, let alone give the right to his followers to reject these men as their leaders. Abraham tried to fulfill God's covenant on his own, fathering a child (Ishmael) with Hagar, his wife's maidservant, instead of trusting that God would miraculously provide a child through his barren wife Sarah, with whom he ultimately procreated Isaac (Gen. 15—18). There would be significant fallout over time between Isaac and Ishmael and

---

the Protestant groups that have progressively split off therefrom over the centuries. From this perspective, the 33,000 figure may be overstated, but not by a great deal. See Catholic apologist Dave Armstrong's analysis at http://www.philvaz.com/apologetics/a106.htm. (A Catholic apologist is one who explains and defends Church teaching.) Armstrong notes that the WCE estimate for 2025 is 55,000 Christian denominations. See also Armstrong's "Part I" on this matter; http://www.philvaz.com/apologetics/a120.htm.

Finally, the Catholic Church does not view herself as a denomination, which comes from the Latin "de nomine," i.e., "of the name" Christian, but rather as the one Church that Jesus founded.

their respective descendants, yet Abraham remained God's leader despite his covenantal misstep.

Moses did not obey God in seeking to quench the thirst of the wandering Israelites. He struck a rock twice, instead of simply telling the rock to give forth its water, as God had commanded him (Num. 20). This lack of obedience disqualified Moses from receiving the blessing of entering the Promised Land, and it serves as a general reminder to rely on God and not our own devices. But Moses remained the leader of the Israelites until his death.

And King David, whom the Lord described as "a man after his own heart" (1 Sam. 13:14), committed adultery with Bathsheba and orchestrated her husband's murder on the battlefield. David suffered for his grave wrongdoing, but God did not remove him as the king of Israel (2 Sam. 11—12).

What can we learn from the lives of Abraham, Moses and King David? That the actions of God's human leaders do not ultimately make or break the mission of God's people. God's fidelity, which is divinely guaranteed, is what matters most, and that is why God's people were sustained until the time of Jesus, despite their own and often serious misdeeds, whether by certain leaders or the Israelites in general. If God had decided to wait for a "worthy" leader, the people of God would have wandered aimlessly for centuries until the coming of the Messiah.

Jesus Is the Reason We Have
"A Church for All Seasons"

Similarly, when God becomes man, revealing himself as Jesus Christ, he says that he will make a "New Covenant" (Lk. 22:20) in fulfilling his heavenly Father's plan to save the world (Jn. 3:16–17), *and use human leaders to accomplish that plan*. Jesus conveys that he will restore the kingdom of Israel. Jesus will serve as the king and his apostles the royal stewards of the kingdom after Jesus' return to his Father in heaven (Mt. 19:28; see Lk. 1:30–33). Jesus calls this community of the New Covenant his "Church," which derives from the Greek word *ekklesia*—meaning "assembly"—the Hebrew equivalent of which was used to describe Old Covenant Israel. Jesus establishes his Church on "the rock" of St. Peter, but quickly makes clear that the Church's strength will not be Peter, but rather that he—Jesus—will divinely ensure that "the gates of Hades shall not prevail against it" (Mt. 16:18).[6]

Jesus gives Peter "the keys of the kingdom of heaven" (Mt. 16:19), signaling his future role as the Church's chief shepherd[7] and teacher. He prays for Peter in particular in leading his Church (Lk. 22:31–32), and Peter's primacy can be seen elsewhere, including in overseeing the Council of Jerusalem (Acts 15).

---

[6] "Hades" is another name in the Old Testament for Sheol, the abode of the dead. By extension, Hades is also the realm from which the devil and his demonic minions foster death and deception (see Rev. 6:8; 20:1–15).

[7] Because they receive the keys from Jesus, Peter and his papal successors are the *merely human* chief shepherds of the Church, governing in the name of Jesus, who is the God-man and thus the *ultimate* "chief Shepherd" (1 Pet. 5:4).

As with imperfect leaders in Old Covenant Israel like Moses and David, Popes aren't exempt from personal moral failure. But God sustains them in their leadership, safeguarding them from definitively teaching error on faith and morals despite their personal sins. Moral transgressions should never be taken lightly, especially among the Pope and other Church leaders, as they can be occasions of serious scandal for both Christians and non-Christians (see CCC 2284–87). In the case of a Pope, they could be the cause for his free resignation,[8] and, in the case of leaders under the Roman Pontiff, removal from office. Catholics can take great consolation that Jesus assures Peter and his papal successors that the forces of death and destruction will never prevail over the universal Church, though not necessarily in a particular country or region, where it's possible for the Church to cease to exist.[9]

As we will see more clearly in Chapter 1, Jesus also gives his other apostles authority under the leadership of Peter, and he provides that they will have successors after their deaths, similar to how leadership was sustained in Old Covenant Israel. Suffice it to say for now that Jesus grounds his Church leadership in Peter and the other apostles, giving them the power to forgive sins following his Resurrection. In doing so, Jesus tells his apostles, "As the Father has sent me, even so I send you" (Jn. 20:21). How did the

---

[8] Lest there be any doubt, there was no moral depravity that hastened Pope Benedict XVI's resignation. Age and fatigue were the causes.

[9] This possibility should provide prayerfully sober reflection in countries where the Church's membership has declined significantly in the last several decades.

Father send Jesus? As we learn just prior to Christ's Ascension, Jesus tells his apostles, "All authority in heaven and on earth has been given to me" (Mt. 28:18). Consequently, in giving his apostles the Great Commission to "make disciples of all nations" (Mt. 28:19), Jesus sends them out with _"all authority in heaven and on earth"_ to teach and govern in his name, so that whatever they bind on earth shall be bound in heaven and whatever they loose on earth will be loosed in heaven (Mt. 28:18, emphasis added; 16:19; 18:15–18).

The Church receives stability and unity from Jesus via the teaching and governing authority of Peter and the other apostles—and their successors—and that authority not only encompasses the apostles' teaching, but also the Church's worship and faith life in general (Acts 2:42; see CCC 815). And we know that the Church's mission extends to every nation, because God's salvific plan is for the whole world (Mt. 28:19). And Jesus prays that his people, his Church, would truly be one, as he and his heavenly Father are one (Jn. 17:20–23), a reminder that the Church cannot achieve and sustain that oneness or unity through human effort alone. Rather, Jesus establishes and preserves _visible_ structures of authority in his Church, which even those who are less educated but of goodwill can discern. Without those divine guarantees, the Catholic Church would've been out of business centuries ago, because of attacks both from without and within her membership.

Luther and Calvin Quickly Realize the Need for a Pope, Church Hierarchy

Unfortunately, in his zeal to combat the abuse of indulgences[10] by certain unscrupulous members of the Church, Martin Luther, an Augustinian monk in Germany, broke with the Successor of St. Peter altogether, and in the process established a rival church[11] in competition with the one founded by Jesus.

In contrast to the divinely founded teaching authority of the Magisterium, i.e., the Pope and the bishops in union with him, Luther and his co-Reformers proclaimed "*sola Scriptura,*" the belief that "Scripture alone" is the infallible rule of faith for Christian doctrine and practice, and thus the final court of appeal for adjudicating all matters related to Gospel faith and morality. And so every doctrine, practice or authority must be subject to the authority of Scripture.[12]

---

[10] Indulgences remit the "temporal punishment" of already forgiven sin, punishments which include our painful purification from our "unhealthy attachment to creatures" and other created things (CCC 1472). The Church's doctrine on indulgences will be addressed in Chapter 6.

[11] The word "church" is used loosely here, i.e., in the modern sense. In the strict Catholic doctrinal sense, a "church" refers only to those Christian entities that are headed by a validly ordained bishop, e.g., Catholic and Orthodox churches. The word "churches" can be used in a legitimate, lowercased way among Catholics when referring collectively to various dioceses, which are each headed by their respective bishops and are all in communion with the Pope in the one, universal Church.

[12] For more on a Protestant perspective regarding *sola Scriptura,* see Norman L. Geisler and Ralph E. MacKenzie, "What Is *Sola Scriptura?*"; http://www.equip .org/article/what-is-sola-scriptura/; and "A Defense of *Sola Scriptura*"; http://ww w.equip.org/article/a-defense-of-sola-scriptura/. See also "*Sola Scriptura:* What

But the inherent unworkability of *sola Scriptura*—and therefore the need for an ultimate authority over Church teaching and other governance—quickly became evident among the earliest Protestant Reformers. When Luther had a disagreement about the nature of the Eucharist with the Swiss Reformer Ulrich Zwingli, it soon became clear that someone needed to have final authority to determine who was right and who was wrong. And the mediating efforts of the irenic Martin Bucer, who favored Zwingli's view, were not sufficient to avoid a split.[13]

John Calvin, another major early Reformer, also experienced the frustration of attempting to operate a church without a Pope and the unity-preserving bishops in union with him. As historian Dr. David Anders[14] observes, Calvin replaced the Pope's teaching authority with his own in authoring *The Institutes of the Christian Religion.* Calvin moved to Geneva, Switzerland, Anders writes, and he used the local city council to first impose a confession of faith—written by Calvin—on the local citizens, and then to erect an ecclesiastical court "to judge the moral and theological purity of his parishioners. . . . Calvin's *Institutes* would eventually be declared official doctrine."[15]

Does *Sola Scriptura* Mean?"; http://www.equip.org/perspectives/sola-scriptura-what-does-sola-scriptura-mean/.

[13] The respective views of Luther and Zwingli on the Eucharist will be covered in Chapter 4.

[14] Anders is a Catholic convert from Calvinism.

[15] A. David Anders, Ph.D., "How John Calvin Made Me a Catholic," June 1, 2010, emphasis original; http://www.calledtocommunion.com/2010/06/how-john-calvin-made-me-a-catholic/.

And yet for all of Calvin's "passion for order and author-ity," Anders concludes that Calvin

> had rejected any rational or consistent basis for that authority. He knew that Scripture *totally* alone, Scripture interpreted by each individual conscience, was a recipe for disaster. But his own claim to authority was perfectly arbitrary. . . . John Calvin had high expectations for the unity and catholicity of the faith, and for the centrality of Church and sacrament. But Calvinism couldn't deliver it. Outside of Geneva, without the force of the state to impose one version, Calvinism it-self splintered into factions. . . . His own followers descended into anarchy and individualism.[16]

Indeed, the Reformation's beginnings reaffirm that *some-body* has to interpret and safeguard Scripture authorita-tively. The actions of the two most important and influen-tial Reformers—Luther and Calvin—clearly illustrate that. The Bible, like the U.S. Constitution, cannot interpret it-self. In addition, Luther, Zwingli and Bucer were all Catho-lic priests. They were not the descendants of some faithful early-Church remnant. And so they found themselves in a classic "Catch 22" scenario, even if they didn't recog-nize it at the time. That is, either the Catholic Church is right and they were wrong in breaking with the Church, or they were right in claiming that the Catholic Church had taught various doctrinal errors for almost 1,500 years. If the Church has fallen into error, though, that would also mean that the gates of hell have prevailed against the Church, contrary to what Jesus promised (see Mt. 16:18) and thereby undermining his claims to divinity.

---

[16] Ibid.

What *Did* Jesus Do?

So a crisis of authority is evident in the very beginnings of the Reformation, a crisis which Protestantism has not been able to overcome and, indeed, cannot overcome given its lack of a centralized teaching authority provided by God; and because of its rejection of various teachings, the assent to which Christ has made a normative part of humanity's salvation.[17]

---

[17] God calls everyone to the fullness of truth and grace in his one Catholic Church as the "normative" or standard way of salvation. In addition, "all salvation comes from Christ the Head through the Church which is his Body" (CCC 846). Thus, Christ desires that *all* people be saved (1 Tim. 2:4), whether Orthodox and Protestant Christians, (CCC 838), non-Christians (CCC 839–43) or nonbelievers. The *Catechism of the Catholic Church* summarizes:

> [T]hey could not be saved who, knowing that the Catholic Church was founded as necessary by God through Christ, would refuse either to enter it or to remain in it (CCC 846, citing Vatican II, *Lumen Gentium* [LG] 14, emphasis added). . . .

> [Yet,] those who, *through no fault of their own*, do not know the Gospel of Christ or his Church, but who nevertheless seek God with a sincere heart, and, moved by grace, try in their actions to do his will as they know it through the dictates of their conscience—those too may achieve eternal salvation (CCC 847, citing LG 16, emphasis added; see CCC 1257). . . .

> [Still,] although in ways known to himself God can lead those who, through no fault of their own, are ignorant of the Gospel, to that faith without which it is impossible to please him, *the Church still has the obligation and also the sacred right to evangelize all men* (CCC 848, citing Vatican II, *Ad Gentes* [AG] 7, emphasis added).

In summary, Catholics should not presume upon their own salvation, lest they be not only eternally lost but also "the more severely judged" for squandering an abundance of graces that Christ makes available to them in his Church (LG 14). Similarly, the Church should not presume upon the salvation of any non-Catholic. As the Vatican II Council Fathers soberly observed:

> [O]ften men, *deceived by the Evil One*, have become vain in their reasonings and have exchanged the truth of God for a lie, serving the creature rather

Sola Scriptura is also shown to be faulty in that the canon —or list of books—of the New Testament was not initially canonized[18] until the late fourth century, illustrating that it was the Church who determined the canon of the Bible under the guidance of the Holy Spirit. Early Christian writings outnumbered the 27 books that would become the canon of the New Testament. The shepherds of the Church, by a process of spiritual discernment and investigation into the liturgical traditions of the Church spread throughout the world, had to draw clear lines of distinction between books that are truly inspired by God and originated in the apostolic period, and those which only claimed to have these qualities.

To be sure, the Bible is not a self-canonizing collection of books. Rather, living persons external to the Bible, guided by Jesus and the Holy Spirit (see Jn. 16:13), were needed to undertake the effort of selecting and excluding would-be biblical books. In addition, that the New Testament canon wasn't settled until the late 300s further testifies to the importance of the apostles and their successors—as well as the teaching of the apostles—in sustaining the life of the early Church. This life included the proclamation of approved sacred writings, e.g., excerpts from the four Gospels and the letters of St. Paul, in the Church's regular worship, i.e., liturgy.

---

than the Creator. Or some there are who, living and dying in this world without God, *are exposed to final despair. Wherefore to promote the glory of God and procure the salvation of all of these, and mindful of the command of the Lord, "Preach the Gospel to every creature,"* the Church fosters the missions *with care and attention* (LG 16, emphases added).

[18] That is, formally decreed by Church authority to be part of the New Testament canon.

In summary, everything about the Catholic Church is rooted in Jesus and his actions. Catholics believe in the Church because Jesus founded it (see Mt. 16:16–19; see 1 Tim. 3:15). Catholics respect and submit to the Pope, because he is "_the_ Vicar of Christ," i.e., the priestly Successor of St. Peter who definitively teaches and governs in Christ's name because he is sustained by the Holy Spirit, whom Jesus sent to lead his Church into all truth (Jn. 16:13; see Lk. 10:16). Catholics honor and seek the assistance of Mary, because she is the Mother of God (see Lk. 1:43), as well as the other saints, because they are alive to God in heaven (see Mt. 22:31–32). Despite distortions of Church teaching and missteps of Church leaders and rank-and-file Catholics over the centuries, the genius of Catholicism—the authentic power and mission of the Catholic Church—will always be found in Jesus Christ, who established the Church, his Mystical Body[19] or bride,[20] as "the universal sacrament of salvation."[21]

The balance of this book will further endeavor to show how Jesus accomplishes his saving mission, including by our acceptance of his liberating truth, which is contained in both sacred Scripture and sacred Tradition (see CCC 74–90), as well as by our living out that truth, particularly in the celebration of the sacraments—and especially the Sacrifice of the Mass—in communion with the Blessed Mother, the angels and all of the other saints.

---

[19] See 1 Cor. 12:12–26; Rom. 12:15.

[20] Eph. 5:25–32.

[21] Vatican II, LG 48; http://www.vatican.va/archive/hist_councils/ii_vatican_council/documents/vat-ii_const_19641121_lumen-gentium_en.html.

1

"He Who Hears You Hears Me"
(Luke 10:16)

God's Use of Human Leaders throughout Salvation History

God does not abandon his people. This is a theme that runs throughout salvation history. Even when his people sin, God seeks to reconcile them to himself, and any discipline he administers is meant to be remedial, to help his people learn from their transgressions and seek to regain fruitful fellowship with him. Chastisement is an expression of love, as every parent who disciplines their children understands, even if the children may not immediately appreciate the correction.

We see this initially with Adam and Eve, our first parents. When they fail to trust God and transgress the First Commandment, yielding to the devil's temptation, God does not abandon them. Their life is made difficult because of the consequences of their sin and their relationship with God becomes more distant (CCC 374–79; 402–6). But God refuses to give up on Adam and Eve and withdraw from them completely. Instead, he gives them hope that their descendants will prevail in their battle against the devil:

I will put enmity between you and the woman, and between your seed and her seed; he shall bruise your head, and you shall bruise his heel (Gen. 3:15).

The Church has traditionally viewed this passage as the _Protoevangelium_ ("first Gospel"), a prophecy of the Good News that the Messiah and his Blessed Mother Mary will vanquish the devil and put an end to sin and death (see 1 Cor. 15:45; Rom. 5:12–18). Because God loves us, he gives each of us a free will, allowing us to freely choose to serve him or not. For love coerced is not love at all. Yet, while permitting our first parents to accept or reject him, God shows his love further by revealing a plan to redeem mankind. Indeed, God loves us too much to let us go without doing everything possible to bring us back. That's why Jesus comes to provide us with something much greater: the infinite mercy of God that leads us to eternal life in heaven with him (CCC 410–12). Sin never has the last word with God.

When we look at salvation history, we see that God raises up leaders to play a part in reconciling man with himself. The Book of Genesis shows us that God called Abram to begin to reverse the damage caused by Adam's sin and help ultimately return the human family to a state of blessing. God calls Abram, which means "exalted father," from Ur of the Chaldeans (modern-day Iraq), and leads him to a region that will become the Promised Land of Israel:

Go from your country and your kindred and your father's house to the land that I will show you. And I will make of you a great nation, and I will bless you, and make your name great, so that you will be a blessing. I will bless those who bless you, and him who curses you I will curse; and by you all the families of the earth shall bless themselves (Gen. 12:1–3).[1]

God makes a covenant with Abram to form a great nation with his descendants, a multitude too numerous to number (Gen. 15). Abram believes God (Gen. 15:6), but then later laughs because not only are he and his wife Sarai still childless when God reaffirms his sacred vow, but Sarai is well beyond child-bearing years at age 90 and he is now 100! (Gen. 17:17).

Abram, seeing the barrenness of his elderly wife, falters in his trust of God and fathers a son, Ishmael, through his wife's maidservant, Hagar (Gen. 16). Yet God remains true to his word, not rejecting Abram but changing his name to "Abraham" ("father of a multitude"), because he will become "the father of a multitude of nations" (Gen. 17:5). God makes another covenant with Abraham, saying that kings will come forth from him (Gen. 17:6–7). With these words, God foretells the kingdom of David, with whom he would establish an everlasting covenant (2 Sam. 7:12–19). This kingdom is ultimately fulfilled in Jesus, a descendant of David, who will ascend to David's throne and reconstitute the Davidic kingdom as the angel Gabriel tells Mary (Lk. 1:30–33).

At long last, the elderly Abraham and Sarah[2] have a son,

---

[1] Abram was 75 when he was first called by God (Gen. 12:4).

[2] Sarah's name was originally "Sarai," which means "my princess." Her name was changed (Gen. 17:15) along with her husband's. "Sarah," as the *Jewish Encyclopedia* provides, means simply "princess," because she would now be recognized generally as such. See http://www.jewishencyclopedia.com/articles/13194-sarah-sarai.

Isaac, and then God tests Abraham's faith again. Isaac was Abraham's only son according to God's covenantal plan (see Gen. 22:1–2), the son through whom God would bless all nations, i.e., provide a universal or "catholic" blessing to the whole world (see Gen. 12:3). And yet God directs Abraham to offer Isaac as a sacrifice, though intervenes when Abraham shows radical trust. As the Letter to the Hebrews says, the patriarch believed that God would raise Isaac from the dead (Heb. 11:17–19). Abraham and Isaac thereby become prophetic symbols or types of God the Father and Jesus because, later on in salvation history, the Father will send his only Son to die as a Sacrifice to atone for all of mankind's sins (Jn. 3:16–17). And so, after testing Abraham, God reaffirms that he will bless all of the nations of the earth through Abraham's descendants (Gen. 22:15–18).

Fidelity to Moses (and God's Other Commissioned Leaders): An Extension of Faithfulness to God

The patriarchs Isaac and Jacob descend from Abraham, and God renames Jacob "Israel" (Gen. 32:28),[3] from which we derive the name "Israelites." Eventually, God raises up a new leader, Moses, who guides the Israelites out of bondage in Egypt, and with whom God seals a covenant to form the nation of Israel (Ex. 24). Two events in Moses' life illustrate the importance of remaining faithful to God's commissioned leaders, *not* because they are necessarily the best

---

[3] The verse is 32:29 in the New American Bible.

and holiest people *but simply because God has commissioned them*. Fidelity to God's leaders ultimately becomes a test of obedience to God.

In the first event Miriam and Aaron, Moses' sister and brother, speak against Moses because he marries Zipporah (Ex. 2:20–22). She was not an Israelite but rather a Cushite, Cush corresponding to modern-day Ethiopia. Because of their narrow, nationalistic view of who could be included in God's people (Num. 12:1), they say, "Has the Lord indeed spoken only through Moses? Has he not spoken through us also?" (Num. 12:2). As a punishment, Miriam is struck with leprosy, her skin ironically becoming "white as snow" (Num. 12:10). Aaron and Miriam repent of their sins, and they serve as examples of the peril that comes with conspiring against God's commissioned leaders.

The second event is even more dramatic. In Numbers 16, Korah, Dathan and Abiram lead a rebellion against the leadership of Moses, as well as Aaron, who along with his descendants served as Old Covenant Levitical priests (Ex. 40:12–15). If you've seen the epic film *The Ten Commandments*, the name "Dathan" may ring a bell. He was played by Edward G. Robinson, whose cinematic portrayal includes presenting Dathan as a traitorous Israelite who collaborated with the enemy Egyptians. In the movie as well, Dathan, Korah and Abiram's rebellion against Moses is conflated with the worship of the Golden Calf (Ex. 32).

As a descendant of Levi—though not in the line of Aaron—Korah and his fellow Levites provide liturgical assistance with the wilderness tabernacle (Ex. 32:29), a forerunner to the Temple in Jerusalem, but they also desire the priesthood, i.e., the leading liturgical role in Israelite worship. And Dathan and Abiram, descendants of Reuben,[4] complain because the Israelites had left bountiful Egypt, a land flowing with milk and honey, and hadn't reached the Promised Land. Instead, they were struggling in the wilderness. The three rebels speak against Moses and Aaron: "You have gone too far! For all the congregation are holy, every one of them, and the LORD is among them; why then do you exalt yourselves above the assembly of the LORD?" (Num. 16:3).

Notice how they sound like Miriam and Aaron? Korah, Dathan and Abiram presume to exalt themselves over and against the ones whom God has exalted. Moses and Aaron were called and commissioned by the Lord for religious leadership; the others were not. It's the difference between divine promotion and self-promotion. In exalting themselves, they set themselves against God. But, unlike Aaron and Miriam, they refuse to repent. So Moses separates the rest of the Israelites from those who had allied themselves with Korah, Dathan and Abiram, who were about to learn the very hard way, as Jesus would later say, that "whoever exalts himself will be humbled" (Mt. 23:12):

> And Moses said, "Hereby you shall know that the LORD has sent me to do all these works, and that it has not been of my own accord. If these men die the common death of all men, or if they are visited by the fate of all men, then the LORD has not sent me. But if the LORD creates something new, and the ground opens its mouth, and swallows them up, with all that belongs to them, and they go down alive into

---

[4] Levi and Reuben are two of the sons of the great patriarch Jacob/Israel, and so their descendants form two of the 12 tribes of Israel.

Sheol, then you shall know that these men have despised the LORD."

And as he finished speaking all these words, the ground under them split asunder; and the earth opened its mouth and swallowed them up, with their households and all the men that belonged to Korah and all their goods. So they and all that belonged to them went down alive into Sheol; and the earth closed over them, and they perished from the midst of the assembly. And all Israel that were round about them fled at their cry; for they said, "Lest the earth swallow us up!" And fire came forth from the LORD, and consumed the two hundred and fifty men offering the incense (Num. 16:28–35).[5]

In this passage, the rebels are collectively represented by Korah, since he led the rebellion. In the New Testament, Korah receives a single but important mention in the Letter of Jude. Jude warns a community of Christians against false leaders who operate in the immoral tradition of Korah and his confreres: "Woe to them! For they walk in the way of Cain, and abandon themselves for the sake of gain to Balaam's error, and perish in Korah's rebellion" (Jude 11).

As in ancient Israel, so too with Christ's Church in the New Covenant: Jude makes clear that God commissions men to lead his people, and those who oppose his leaders, whatever their good intentions may be, objectively set themselves up against God and his saving plan, and thereby put themselves and others in spiritual peril.

---

[5] The 250 men had joined the rebellion of Korah, Dathan and Abiram (Num. 16:2, 16–18).

Nothing Succeeds Like Succession: Passing on Authority among God's People

Eventually, God fulfills his covenant with Abraham to make a great kingdom of his descendants. David is God's choice to lead his people. But David doesn't rule by himself. He has royal courtiers who assist in the administration of his kingdom, the most important of whom was "the master of the palace"[6] or chief steward over David's kingdom. This man would exercise royal authority in the name of the king. The prophet Isaiah notes the importance of this royal office in discussing how the righteous Eliakim succeeds the corrupt Shebna:

> Thus says the LORD God of hosts, "Come, go to this steward, to Shebna, who is over the household, and say to him: What have you to do here and whom have you here, that you have hewn here a tomb for yourself, you who hew a tomb on the height, and carve a habitation for yourself in the rock? Behold, the LORD will hurl you away violently, O you strong man. . . . I will thrust you from your office, and you will be cast down from your station. In that day I will call my servant Eliakim the son of Hilkiah, and I will clothe him with your robe, and will bind your belt on him, and will commit your authority to his hand; and he shall be a father to the inhabitants of Jerusalem and to the house of Judah. And I will place on his shoulder the key of the house of David; he shall open, and none shall shut; and he shall shut, and none shall open" (Is. 22:15–17, 19–22).

A few important points jump out in this passage from the Book of Isaiah. Shebna is corrupt, but his corruption

---

[6] Isaiah 22:15, as rendered in the New American Bible.

means he will be replaced, *not* that his office will be discontinued. Here we see an important Old Testament precedent for succession, as Eliakim takes his place. In addition, Eliakim is no ordinary royal courtier. He has the key of the house of David, exercising power in the king's name in meting out justice and mercy through "opening" and "shutting." Finally, Eliakim will be "a father" to those who live in Jerusalem, i.e., the capital of David's kingdom.

The King of Kings, His Men and His Main Man

The Davidic kingdom would fall in 586 B.C.,[7] when the Babylonians destroyed the Temple and Jerusalem. But the kingdom would be restored in connection with a "New Covenant" (Jer. 31:31–34). And when Jesus comes to reconstitute the Davidic kingdom, as Gabriel promised (see Lk. 1:31–33), there will be only one king, not a succession of kings. That's because Jesus, who is both God and man, is "the King of kings and the Lord of lords" who will reign forever (Rev. 17:14; 19:16; see 1 Tim. 6:15).

As a new and greater David (Mt. 21:9), Jesus also commissions royal stewards to oversee his kingdom on earth. The Old Covenant kingdom was founded on the 12 tribes of Israel, whereas Jesus establishes the New Covenant Israel on the leadership of his Twelve Apostles (Lk. 22:28–30). Any messenger Jesus commissions speaks in his name, including the 70 he appoints to proclaim his kingdom: "He who hears you hears me, and he who rejects you rejects me,

---

[7] Some scholars date the destruction of Jerusalem to 587 B.C.

and he who rejects me rejects him who sent me" (Lk. 10:16). Yet, to his apostles, Jesus gives an even greater leadership role, commissioning them to make disciples of the whole world through preaching, teaching and baptizing (Mt. 28:18–20).

In governing Christ's kingdom on earth, however, only one would have primacy under the leadership of Christ the King.[8] As with Eliakim in relation to his fellow courtiers, only Peter among the apostles is given keys, but his are the "keys of the kingdom of heaven." Consequently, in emulating but exceeding Eliakim's governing power to open and shut, Peter has the power to bind and loose, and Jesus assures him that "whatever you bind on earth will be bound in heaven, and whatever you loose on earth will be loosed in heaven" (Mt. 16:19).

I remember interacting with an Independent Baptist minister who said that once you've poured the foundation of a building, you don't keep pouring it. He said that Jesus gave Peter an initial leadership role in getting the Church started, but Jesus didn't establish the papacy and so Peter had no successor. I engaged his construction analogy, arguing that not recognizing the papacy—and therefore Peter's successors—would be like yanking out the foundation of a building instead of continuing to build on it.

If the royal steward overseeing the Old Covenant kingdom of Israel had successors to continue advancing the

---

[8] While Peter and his papal successors have supreme authority among the Catholic faithful in governing the Church on earth, Jesus _delegates_ his authority to the Pope, for Christ the King has ultimate control over the keys of his kingdom (see Rev. 3:7).

kingdom, how much more would successors be needed to oversee and advance the kingdom of heaven, which reaches throughout the whole world and beyond? While a successor to Peter is not named in the Bible, we have other solid evidence that Jesus ensured that this leadership parallel would endure in the New Covenant. For example, there is ample and reliable historical testimony that Peter had papal successors, including Linus, Cletus, Clement, Sixtus, etc.[9]

In addition, Acts 1 illustrates that the apostle Judas, who had sadly taken his life, had a successor in Matthias (Acts 1:20–28). And if a successor for Judas, again, how much more need would there be to replace the leader of the Apostles, St. Peter? Also, in his *Letter to the Corinthians* in the late first century, Pope St. Clement, the fourth Pope, makes clear that *all* of the apostles possessed offices of succession.[10] Furthermore, similar to his Old Covenant

---

[9] See, for example, St. Irenaeus, *Against Heresies*, bk. 3, ch. 3, sect. 3; http://www.newadvent.org/fathers/0103303.htm. See also "Chronological Lists of Popes," *The Catholic Encyclopedia* (New York: The Encyclopedia Press, Inc., 1913); http://www.newadvent.org/cathen/12272a.htm.

[10] Pope St. Clement writes, "Our apostles knew from our Lord Jesus Christ that there would be contention over the title of the bishop's office. For this reason, having received perfect foreknowledge, they appointed those mentioned before and afterwards gave the provision that, if they should fall asleep, other approved men would succeed their ministry" (*Letter to the Corinthians*, ch. 44, sects. 1–2). As cited in Kenneth J. Howell, *Clement of Rome and the Didache: A New Translation and Theological Commentary* (Zanesville, OH: CHResources, 2012), 117.

Apostles were known in Greek as "*epískopoi*," which translates into English as "overseers" or "bishops" (Phil. 1:1; 1 Tim. 3:1). All Catholic bishops today serve in an unbroken lineage of apostolic succession that begins with the Twelve Apostles. And there is a complete list of the Popes, the Successors of St. Peter. See http://www.ewtn.com/holysee/Pontiff/popesall.asp.

predecessors, Peter is a "Holy Father" or "Pope" to the inhabitants of the New Covenant Jerusalem or kingdom of Israel.

Some Protestant Christians argue that Jesus built the Church on himself, citing St. Paul, who refers to Jesus as the cornerstone of the Church (Eph. 2:20). In the original New Testament Greek, they add, St. Matthew presents Jesus as saying, "And I tell you, you are Peter [*Petros*—Greek: "small stone"] and on this rock [*petra*—Greek: "massive rock," i.e., Jesus] I will build my Church" (Mt. 16:18). According to this view, the Gospel writer is distinguishing small, weak Peter and the divinely powerful Jesus who, again, is the cornerstone.[11] But Jesus spoke Aramaic, not Greek, and the related biblical evidence illustrates that Peter is indeed the rock upon which the Church was built:

> In this language, the word *kepha* is the equivalent of *Peter* and denotes a "sizeable rock"[12]—one suitable for a building foundation. This Aramaic name is preserved as "Cephas"[13] nine times in the NT (Jn. 1:42; 1 Cor. 1:12; 15:5; Gal. 1:18; 2:9, etc.).[14]

---

[11] Others argue that *petra* also refers to Peter's faith, meaning that his belief is what matters, not that Peter had primacy among the Twelve Apostles, let alone apostolic successors in leading the Church.

[12] *Kepha* can also mean "crag," i.e., a steep or rugged cliff or rock face.

[13] Cephas is the Greek transliteration of *kepha* as seen in John 1:42 and elsewhere. For more on this subject, see the Catholic Answers tract "Peter and the Papacy"; http://www.catholic.com/tracts/peter-and-the-papacy.

[14] "Word Study: Peter," *The Ignatius Catholic Study Bible New Testament* (San Francisco: Ignatius Press, 2010), 37.

In addition, Catholic apologist[15] Karl Keating notes that you can't ascribe a feminine name, "*petra*," to an adult male, or any male for that matter:

> In Aramaic the word *kepha* has the same ending whether it refers to a rock or is used as a man's name. In Greek, though, the word for rock, *petra*, is feminine in gender. The translator could use it for the second appearance of *kepha* in the sentence [in Mt. 16:18], but not the first, because it would be inappropriate to give a man a feminine name. So he put a masculine ending on it, and there was *Petros*, which happened to be a preexisting word meaning a small stone. Some of the effect of the play on words was lost, but that was the best that could be done in Greek. In English, as in Aramaic, there is no problem with endings, so an English rendering could read: "Thou art Rock, and upon this rock I will build my Church." In modern French Bibles, the word *pierre* appears in both places. The real meaning is hard to miss.[16]

The use of Cephas throughout the New Testament leaves no doubt that Peter is the rock on which Jesus builds his Church. In addition, Peter's name change from "Simon" confirms his primary leadership role, harking back to the name change of two great patriarchs in the Old Testament—"Abram" to "Abraham" (Gen. 17:5) and "Jacob" to "Israel" (Gen. 32:28)[17]—when they were called by God to serve as great leaders. Jesus is undoubtedly the cornerstone, the God-man without whom the Church could not

---

[15] A Catholic apologist is one who explains and defends Church teaching.

[16] Karl Keating, *Catholicism and Fundamentalism: The Attack on "Romanism" by "Bible Christians"* (San Francisco: Ignatius Press, 1988), 210.

[17] Again, the verse is 32:29 in the New American Bible.

exist. But he builds his Church "upon the foundation of the apostles" (Eph. 2:19–20), all of whom have the power to bind and loose (Mt. 18:15–18) under the leadership of Peter, who alone has the keys of the kingdom of heaven.

In the end, "the buck has to stop" with someone as the saying goes, whether in leading a family, a company or a country. In the Catholic Church, Jesus designates Peter and his successors to have that primacy of authority. Popes are not morally perfect; some have even caused scandal. But Jesus protects all of them from definitively teaching error on matters of faith and morals,[18] and he prevents the gates of hell from prevailing against the Church otherwise (Mt. 16:18). Peter and his papal successors are undoubtedly the chief shepherds[19] of Christ's Church, as Dr. Kenneth Howell further affirms in analyzing the original Greek text of Luke 22:31–32:

---

[18] In 1928, renowned canon lawyer Franz Wernz argued that "a Pope who falls into public heresy would by that fact cease to be a member of the Church; therefore he would also, upon that fact, cease to be the head of Church." As cited in Dr. Edward Peters, "A Canonical Primer on Popes and Heresy," December 16, 2016; https://canonlawblog.wordpress.com/2016/12/16/a-canonical-primer-on-popes-and-heresy/. To be clear, Peters himself has not taken a stand on whether a Pope can automatically fall from office. I too have questions, including who decides whether a Pope has done so, and how? There are definitely perils to alleged sedevacantism, i.e., arguing that a Pope is no longer the Pope because of alleged public heresy. What is not in doubt, given the Church's charism of infallibility, is that the Holy Spirit will prevent a Pope from teaching error via a _definitive act_ or _solemn definition_. A solemn definition can be done by the Pope himself or with his fellow bishops in an ecumenical council (see CCC 890–91; 2035).

[19] See footnote 7 of the Introduction.

Here Jesus singles out Peter for a special role, "Simon, Simon! Satan has sought to sift you (plural) like wheat. But I have prayed for you (singular) so that your (singular) faith not fail. And when you (singular) are turned around, strengthen your brothers." If Satan's desire was to destroy all Apostles (you plural), why would Jesus only pray for Peter (you singular)? The answer is there for all to see. Peter will serve as the encourager of his fellow apostles. This is the exact role for Peter's successors, the bishops of Rome. The Roman bishop (or Pope) is there to strengthen his brothers; they must be united with him.[20]

---

[20] Kenneth J. Howell, *There is Something Greater Here* (Zanesville, OH: CHResources, 2015), 60.

2

Knowing God's Saving Word

The Bible Alone?
Or Scripture, Tradition and the Magisterium?

The Son of God became man and "gave himself as a ransom for all" because, as St. Paul writes, "he desires all men to be saved and to come to the knowledge of the truth" (1 Tim. 2:6, 4). St. John affirms in his Gospel this fundamental truth about Jesus Christ and his mission, in a passage made more famous by its proclamation on signs seen at many sporting events: "For God so loved the world that he gave his only-begotten Son, that whoever believes in him should not perish but have eternal life. For God sent the Son into the world, not to condemn the world, but that the world might be saved through him" (Jn. 3:16–17).[1]

Jesus Christ claims he is "the way, and the truth, and the life"; and that "no one comes to the Father, but by me" (Jn. 14:6). He also tells his followers, "If you continue in my word, you are truly my disciples, and you will know the truth, and the truth will make you free" (Jn. 8:31–32). So God the Father and Jesus clearly desire that we spend eternal life with them in heaven, *not* be separated from them for all eternity in hell (see CCC 1042–50; 1033–37).

---

[1] The signs typically just say "John 3:16."

What _Did_ Jesus Do?

These words of Jesus prompt questions: How do we know the Gospel,[2] i.e., the collective saving truth of Jesus, so that we ourselves can be saved? What ways did Jesus and his disciples use to communicate his truth? And what, if any, institutions did Jesus set up to make sure that his saving truth was faithfully communicated and safeguarded? The answers to these questions are _crucial_, because if what Jesus says about himself is true, then faithfully transmitting the Gospel is _nothing less_ than accurately proclaiming and preserving the meaning of life for all of humanity.

Christians call "the rule of faith" the standard or norm God provides so that his disciples know what to believe, i.e., his saving truth. Protestants believe that the Bible is the sole standard by which the faithful can apprehend God's saving truth and thus the only measuring rod by which to judge any belief or moral behavior. For them, the Bible is the sole and exclusive record of all that Christians believe, and it mandates all that is expected of them. _Sola Scriptura_ ("The Bible alone") became a battle cry for the Reformation. In contrast, the official teaching of the Church based on Scripture and Tradition[3] is the Catholic rule of faith.[4]

---

[2] Here I use "Gospel" more broadly, as the collective Christian message, instead of one of the four written Gospels of the New Testament.

[3] The term "Apostolic Tradition" (CCC 75–76) can refer to _both_ (1) written Tradition (Scripture) _and_ (2) unwritten Tradition, which includes the apostles' teaching, liturgical practice and institutions like apostolic succession; or it can refer to _either one_. When the word Tradition is used as a standalone herein, it will refer to unwritten forms of Tradition.

[4] Fr. John Hardon, S.J., provides further help, explaining that the rule of faith is "the norm that enables the faithful to know what to believe. The revealed Word of God in Sacred Scripture and Sacred Tradition is a remote rule of faith. But the teaching of the Church based on divine revelation [i.e., Scripture and Tradition] is the immediate rule of faith"; (Hardon, _Pocket Catholic Dictionary_

The Magisterium is the Church's centralized teaching authority under the leadership of Peter and successive Popes, which Catholics believe Jesus established to faithfully interpret and safeguard that collective saving truth found in Scripture and Tradition, which is known as the "deposit of faith" (CCC 84).

Follow the Leader: Letting Jesus Guide Us in Understanding Him and His Word

In considering a passage we used to open this chapter, John 14:6, notice that Jesus says *he* is the way, the truth and the life. *He* is the fulfillment of God's plan. Following his words, emulating his example, believing in him as Lord and Savior —this is our sure path to eternal life. Jesus' words here indicate that, among the New Testament books, we should listen very closely to *his* words spoken directly to his apostles and other disciples during his earthly ministry, as recorded in the four Gospels. The truth of the New Testament books is also guaranteed by the Holy Spirit's inspiration of their respective authors (CCC 105–8). Yet, we must remember that St. Peter, St. Paul, et al., are disciples of Jesus and not vice versa. So contrary to how some Protestants[5] approach the Bible, St. Paul's letters, for example, should be read

---

[New York: Image Books, 1985], 377). So the Catholic rule of faith is the dynamic fruit of a divinely guided interaction between the Magisterium, Scripture and Tradition. See also, Vatican II, *Dei Verbum* (DV) 8–10, 21.

[5] Protestantism is by nature not monolithic, as there were splits early on in the Reformation, so it's important to qualify doctrines and approaches that not all Protestants embrace. Still, grounding their doctrine in the letters of St. Paul was an early practice among the Reformers and remains so today for many Protestants.

in light of his divine rabbi's words and not the other way around. Interpretations of Paul that are not well-founded on the Gospels can lead to various doctrinal errors, as Peter affirms:

> So also our beloved brother Paul wrote to you according to the wisdom given him, speaking of this as he does in all his letters. There are some things in them hard to understand, which the ignorant and unstable twist to their own destruction, as they do the other Scriptures. You therefore, beloved, knowing this beforehand, beware lest you be carried away with the error of lawless men and lose your own stability (2 Pet. 3:15–17).

And *nowhere* in the Gospels does Jesus say that Sacred Scripture is the one and only source of divine guidance for his disciples. Jesus certainly has great regard for the Scriptures of Israel, i.e., the Old Testament, but he *never* says they will become sufficient when combined one day with the new scriptural writings that he will direct his disciples to write. In fact, Jesus *never* commands his disciples to write new Scriptures, let alone compile them in a "New Testament."

Think about that for a moment. Jesus promises to send the Holy Spirit to lead his apostles, to lead his Church, into all truth (Jn. 16:13). And first recall that Jesus speaks these words to his apostles in the Upper Room at the Last Supper, before his Passion and Death. So the promise to guide "you" into all truth is a promise to the apostolic shepherds of the Church. This is not something Jesus says to the crowds on the hillsides of Galilee, as though every rank-and-file believer is assured of receiving individual divine guidance regarding "all truth."

And Christians believe that one of the ways that God's truth was communicated and recorded was through the writing of the New Testament books. But Jesus never specifies that particular writings by Peter, John, a famous convert who would become known as Paul, etc., would one day comprise his sole, collective saving word. If Jesus intended the Bible to be the one and only rule of faith for the Christian community, we would expect our Savior to instruct his disciples to transcribe his words as a reference point for the New Testament, and to specify which writings by which disciples would eventually be included in this new canon of Scripture. Such a measure would serve well as a preemptive strike against counterfeit gospels and epistles, when the authentic New Testament books were finally written down.

Jesus does *none* of that, however; which should give all Christians—and all non-Christian inquirers as well—pause. Instead, as we saw in the Introduction, Jesus' focus is not on commissioning the writing of books, but on sending his apostles out to make disciples of all nations (Mt. 28:18–20). Jesus tells his apostles, "As the Father has sent me, even so I send you" (Jn. 20:21). And how did the Father send Jesus? Recall Jesus' words just before his Ascension, which we provide now more fully:

> All authority in heaven and on earth has been given to me. Go therefore and make disciples of all nations, baptizing them in the name of the Father and of the Son and of the Holy Spirit, teaching them to observe all that I have commanded you; and behold, I am with you always, to the close of the age (Mt. 28:18–20).

Establishing a Magisterium,
Not Imparting the New Testament

As "the King of kings" (Rev. 17:14), Jesus invests his royal authority in his apostles, an authority that impacts heaven as well as earth, so that whatever they bind on earth will be bound in heaven and whatever they loose on earth will be loosed in heaven (Mt. 16:19; 18:18). That power is undoubtedly exercised in the name of Jesus, who promises to remain with his apostles—and their bishop-successors —until the end of the world (Mt. 28:20). By empowering his apostles to communicate and preserve his word, Jesus establishes the visible office of teaching shepherd, so that all of the faithful—both the learned and the lesser-educated—can readily discern who God's official leaders are, be they alive at the time of Sts. Peter and Paul in the early Church, or centuries later when many other bishops have clearly and validly succeeded his first apostles. As Fr. Arnold Damen, S.J., reasons in a homily he gave in the late nineteenth century:

> If God commands me under pain of eternal damnation to believe all that He has taught, He is bound to give me the means to know what He has taught. And the means that God gives me . . . must be adapted to the capacities of all intellects, must be an infallible means to us, so that if a man makes use of it he will be brought to a knowledge of all the truths that God has taught.[6]

---

[6] Arnold Damen, S.J., _The Church or The Bible_ (Still River, MA: The Slaves of the Immaculate Heart of Mary, 1985), 4.

In other words, if God wants us to believe and live his truth, he needs to make that truth discernible, and the fundamental way he has done so is through the visible leadership of the apostles and their successors. While primitive printing presses existed centuries earlier, it wasn't until 1,400 years after Christ's earthly ministry that Johannes Gutenberg revolutionized printing with the marked development of moveable type.

And literacy then didn't become commonplace until the nineteenth century in the developed world and this past century for less-developed parts of the world. So for centuries copies of the Bible were rare,[7] and then for several more centuries most Christians couldn't read them. For most of Church history, therefore, even attempting to implement *sola Scriptura* wasn't practical for most Christians. The overwhelming majority of the faithful needed lawful Church leaders to proclaim the Bible to them, typically at Mass, *and then explain the meaning of the scriptural readings proclaimed.* (Beautiful art and architecture aided the Church's cause, as even the illiterate could "read" and understand sermons in stone and stained glass.)

Literacy, of course, is not the only thing required to grasp the meaning of the Bible. The Ethiopian eunuch in Acts 8 was literate, and yet he asks for help to understand the Old Testament passage he is reading, a passage in Isaiah 53 foretelling the Passion of Jesus. The deacon Philip[8] doesn't

---

[7] Recall too that the New Testament was not canonized until the late 300s.

[8] One of seven deacons appointed in the early Church (Acts 6:5). He is distinguished from the apostle Philip (Mt. 10:3).

tell him to rely on the Holy Spirit, which, if *sola Scriptura* were sanctioned by Christ, should've been operative for the canon of Scripture that existed at that time, i.e. the Old Testament. Instead, Philip instructs the eunuch on the meaning and truth of the passage, illustrating further the need for a teaching authority to faithfully interpret and safeguard Scripture (Acts 8:26–40).

That's why St. Paul himself, the most prolific New Testament writer, can speak of "the Church of the living God," and not the Bible, as "the pillar and bulwark of truth" (1 Tim. 3:15).

Given the apostles' divinely commissioned authority, we should not be surprised to see that the Christians in the early Church "held steadfastly to the apostles' teachings" (Acts 2:42).

Jesus sanctioned such teaching in the Great Commission (Mt. 28:18–20). And for about 20 years after Jesus' Ascension, the apostles authoritatively preached and taught the Gospel without the aid of any book of the New Testament.[9] This preaching and teaching encompasses not only the apostles' spoken words, but also the example they gave and the institutions they established (CCC 76). Thus, as noted earlier, we can speak of the Church's living Tradition in a larger sense: "[T]he Church, in her doctrine, life and worship, perpetuates and transmits to every generation all that she is, all that she believes" (CCC 78).[10]

---

[9] Paul's First Letter to the Thessalonians is widely believed to be the first New Testament book written—in the early 50s (A.D.).

[10] While citing the *Catechism of the Catholic Church* on Tradition, Dr. David Anders adds, "In the broadest possible sense, Tradition is simply everything that

Apostolic Tradition vs. Human Traditions

This wider sense of Tradition is affirmed in Scripture regarding the early Church: "And they held steadfastly to the apostles' teaching and fellowship, to the breaking of the bread and to the prayers" (Acts 2:42). The four pillars of Catholic catechisms composed throughout Church history are based on this passage: (1) Faith (the apostles' teaching); (2) Liturgy or Sacraments, particularly the Eucharist ("the breaking of the bread" was an early name for the Sacrifice of the Eucharist/Mass);[11] (3) the Christian Moral Life (fellowship); and (4) the Church's rich life of Prayer, beginning with the Lord's Prayer (the prayers).

Despite this biblical evidence, some Protestant Christians argue that Jesus spoke against "tradition." Here we need to distinguish between "Apostolic Tradition" or "Sacred Tradition" and mere "human tradition." The former is established by God; the latter is not, and therefore it can sometimes stand in opposition to the written word of God:

> Then Pharisees and scribes came to Jesus from Jerusalem and said, "Why do your disciples transgress the tradition of the elders? For they do not wash their hands when they eat." He answered them, "And why do you transgress the commandment of God for the sake of your tradition? For God commanded, 'Honor your father and your mother,' and, 'He

---

the Church has and does to transmit the faith from generation to generation. This includes her liturgy, sacraments, canons, devotions, teaching, and preaching . . ." (Anders, "On the Usefulness of Tradition: A Response to Recent Objections," February 8, 2013); http://www.calledtocommunion.com/2013/02/on-the-usefulness-of-tradition-a-response-to-recent-objections/.

[11] See also Acts 20:7, 11; Lk. 24:30–31.

who speaks evil of father or mother, let him surely die.' But you say, 'If any one tells his father or his mother, What you would have gained from me is given to God, he need not honor his father.'[12] So, for the sake of your tradition, you have made void the word of God. You hypocrites! Well did Isaiah prophesy of you, when he said: 'This people honors me with their lips, but their heart is far from me; in vain do they worship me, teaching as doctrines the precepts of men'" (Mt. 15:1–9).

In this passage, Jesus is not ruling out Tradition, i.e., a nonbiblical transmission of his saving truth that he later commissions his apostles to impart. Jesus instead critiques the traditions of the elders (the oral Torah), which the Pharisees placed in competition with Scripture and sometimes even above Scripture, as in this case. It's an example of elevating rabbinic rulings and traditions above the inspired word of God, in this case to relieve a person's sacred obligations to their parents.

As a defense of *sola Scriptura*, some Protestant Christians will cite 2 Timothy 3:16–17: "All scripture is inspired by God and profitable for teaching, for reproof, for correction, and for training in righteousness, that the man of God may be complete, equipped for every good work." Yet, St. Paul's focus to St. Timothy here is squarely on guidance for the moral life—being equipped to do every good work—not on being equipped to know all aspects of Christian belief and practice. Indeed, Paul addresses the privileged role that Scripture plays in training the saints in righteousness, not about its being a final court of appeal for all matters of Christian doctrine and worship.

---

[12] By dedicating their property to God, i.e., to the Temple, a person could

For those who might persist in saying that this passage supports *sola Scriptura*, Blessed John Henry Cardinal Newman has an additional refutation. He notes that if the Protestant argument proves anything it proves too much, because the only Scripture written *and* recognized by the Church when Paul was writing were the Old Testament books, meaning that "the Scriptures of the New Testament were *not* necessary for a rule of faith."[13] Indeed, much of the New Testament had not even been written, let alone formally canonized by the Church as the New Testament, when Paul wrote his Second Letter to Timothy.

Protestant Christians also often cite 1 Corinthians 4:6, in which St. Paul says, "I have applied all this to myself and Apollos for your benefit, brethren, that you may learn by us not to go beyond what is written, that none of you may be puffed up in favor of one against another." But as in 2 Timothy, Paul is referring to the Old Testament Scriptures, in this case their admonitions on humility.[14]

---

sidestep helping their parents, and yet never have to actually give up what they dedicated. This is surely a human tradition worth condemning.

[13] John Henry Newman, *On the Inspiration of Scripture*, eds. J. Derek Holmes and Robert Murray (Washington: Corpus Books, 1967), emphasis added. As cited in Karl Keating, *Catholicism and Fundamentalism: The Attack on "Romanism" by "Bible Christians"* (San Francisco: Ignatius Press, 1988), 136.

[14] Consider this insight on 1 Corinthians 4:6:

Paul cautions believers to stay within the limits of personal humility defined by the Scriptures. He is referring specifically to the string of Old Testament warnings about boasting quoted earlier in the letter (1:19, 31; 3:19–20). Paul's purpose here is to halt the damaging effects of arrogance in Corinth, as indicated by the clarification that follows. Interpretations of this verse that Paul is restricting the basis for Christian doctrine and morals to what is explicitly set forth in the books of the

In contrast, St. Paul affirms the authority of Apostolic Tradition in his Second Letter to the Thessalonians: "So then, brethren, stand firm and hold to the traditions which you were taught by us, _either by word of mouth_ or by letter" (2 Thess. 2:15, emphasis added). And to St. Timothy, "You then, my son, be strong in the grace that is in Christ Jesus, _and what you have heard from me before many witnesses entrust to faithful men who will be able to teach others also_" (2 Tim. 2:1–2, emphasis added; see 1 Cor. 11:2; 15:3). Not only does Paul affirm his own oral teaching, which Timothy heard before many witnesses, but he also tells Timothy to entrust others to share that same teaching.[15]

Sola Scriptura Falls Short

A classic Protestant defense of _sola Scriptura_ is that any Apostolic Tradition that was once oral is _completely_ included in the writings of the New Testament, and therefore what was once Apostolic Tradition is now indistinguishable from the New Testament.[16] The _New Bible Dictionary_ summarizes this perspective:

Bible (_sola Scriptura_) are misleading and untenable. Nothing in the context points to such a broad concern, and in any case Paul insists elsewhere that even the inspired preaching of the apostles is on par with the written word of God (1 Thess. 2:13; 2 Thess. 2:15; 3:6); (_The Ignatius Catholic Study Bible New Testament_ [San Francisco: Ignatius Press, 2010], 289).

[15] For more on this topic, see the Catholic Answers tracts "Scripture and Tradition"; http://www.catholic.com/tracts/scripture-and-tradition; and "Apostolic Tradition"; http://www.catholic.com/tracts/apostolic-tradition.

[16] Of course, even if this could be established as true, it would still not account for the unwritten Tradition regarding liturgical practice, lines of apostolic/episcopal succession, etc.

Apostolic tradition was at one time oral, but for us it is crystallized in the apostolic writing containing the Spirit-guided witness to the Christ of God. Other teaching, while it may be instructive and useful and worthy of serious consideration, cannot claim to be placed alongside the Old Testament and New Testament as authoritative without manifesting the same defect as condemned Jewish tradition in the eyes of our Lord.[17]

In addition, and even though John Calvin tried to be the doctrinal czar of Geneva as we saw in the Introduction, there is allegedly no need for a Magisterium; because, as the Reformer explained, the Holy Spirit infallibly enlightens each Christian believer:

[T]he testimony of the Spirit is superior to reason. For as God alone can properly bear witness to his own words, so these words will not obtain full credit in the hearts of men, until they are sealed by the inward testimony of the Spirit. . . .[18]

Let it therefore be held as fixed, that those who are inwardly taught by the Holy Spirit acquiesce implicitly in Scripture; that Scripture, carrying its own evidence along with it, deigns not to submit to *proofs and arguments*, but owes the full conviction with which we ought to receive it to the testimony of the Spirit. *Enlightened by him, we no longer believe, either on our own Judgment or that of others, that the Scriptures are from God*; but, in a way superior to human Judgment, feel perfectly assured—as much so as if we beheld the divine image visibly

---

[17] *New Bible Dictionary*, 2nd ed., J. D. Douglas, organiz. ed. (Wheaton, IL: Tyndale House, 1984), 1212. As cited in Mark P. Shea, *By What Authority: An Evangelical Discovers Catholic Tradition* (Huntington, IN: Our Sunday Visitor, Inc., 1996), 80.

[18] John Calvin, *The Institutes of the Christian Religion*, trans. Henry Beveridge, bk. 1, ch. 7, sect. 4; https://www.ccel.org/ccel/calvin/institutes.iii.viii.html. To access *The Institutes* more generally, see https://www.ccel.org/ccel/calvin/institutes.toc.html.

impressed on it—that it came to us, by the instrumentality of men, from the very mouth of God. We ask not for proofs or probabilities on which to rest our Judgment, but we subject our intellect and Judgment to it as too transcendent for us to estimate.[19]

Faith and reason—and reason includes the "proofs and arguments" that Calvin criticizes—are not at odds with each other, as Jesus demonstrates in his arguments with the Pharisees (e.g., Mt. 12:1–14), St. Peter also in proclaiming the Gospel on the Day of Pentecost (Acts 2:14–36), and St. Paul further in his preaching to the Athenians (Acts 17:16–36). Appeals to one's faculty of reason —a power every human person has in being made in the image and likeness of God (see Gen. 1:26–27)—is a fundamental part of preaching and defending the faith, as well as in ascertaining meaning when hearing or reading God's word. More to the point, being a baptized Christian, and therefore having the indwelling of the Holy Spirit (see CCC 1265–66), doesn't mean a believer is equipped to infallibly understand Scripture on his own. As St. Peter teaches:

First of all you must understand this, that no prophecy of Scripture is a matter of one's own interpretation, because no prophecy ever came by the impulse of man, but men moved by the Holy Spirit spoke from God (2 Pet. 1:20–21).

St. Peter is speaking to _fellow_ Christians, _not_ non-Christians. In addition, later in the same epistle, recall that Peter says that in St. Paul's letters "there are some things in them hard to understand, which the ignorant and unstable twist to their own destruction, _as they do the other Scriptures_. . . .

---

[19] Ibid., bk. 1, ch. 7, sect. 5; emphases added.

[B]eware lest you be carried away with the error of lawless men and lose your own stability" (2 Pet. 3:16–17, emphasis added). Some Christians sadly went astray in the early Church, e.g., believing that the Son of God did not become man (Docetism) or that Jesus is not actually eternal God (Arianism).

Interpreting the Bible:
Luther and Calvin Can't Agree

In addition, consider the extensive writings of both Calvin and Martin Luther. *The Institutes of the Christian Religion*, Calvin's magnum opus, is well over 500,000 words by itself. And Luther also wrote prolifically, producing more than 50 published volumes. Both men were committed to explaining Scripture to the masses and rebuking those who didn't adhere to their understanding. (In the process, they ironically but understandably developed *their own Lutheran and Calvinist traditions*, respectively, to support *their own* scriptural interpretations. How else could they safeguard what they believed Scripture teaches?) But if, as Calvin argued, the Holy Spirit convicts each and every believer who either reads the Bible—or hears it preached if they're illiterate —*why the need for so much explanatory writing?* And even Luther and Calvin, two very learned men, could not see eye to eye on Scripture and so went their separate ways. Luther, not one to mince words when he opposed someone, described Calvin and his followers as having "in-devilled, over-devilled, and through-devilled hearts."[20]

---

[20] "Martin Luther," *The Catholic Encyclopedia* (New York: The Encyclopedia Press, Inc., 1913); http://www.newadvent.org/cathen/09438b.htm.

If Luther and Calvin, the two most important leaders of the Reformation, couldn't come together on the meaning of Scripture, what was the likelihood that others would? And shouldn't the most influential founders of the Reformation—if it were truly a divine reform—agree, so as to manifest unity in doctrine and Christian life for which Jesus prayed so ardently? (see Jn. 17:20–23). Either the Holy Spirit wasn't doing his job, or Jesus provided a different mechanism for communicating, recording and safeguarding his saving truth. *Precisely because* Jesus prayed that Christians be one like he and his Father are one, you would expect him to provide a clear and reliable means for us to advance and preserve that unity.

The vast writings and other faith-forming efforts of Luther and Calvin further affirm that *someone* needs to interpret Scripture authoritatively, including to bring together the most learned people when they have a doctrinal dispute. Jesus provides the Magisterium—Peter and the apostles in the earliest Church and the Popes and bishops who succeeded them in the centuries that have followed—to teach infallibly on matters of faith and morals under certain conditions (CCC 888–92). The Pope can do so alone when making a solemn definition, though he normally would consult his brother bishops first. And he can do the same with the bishops united with him at an ecumenical council. The most common way, though, is through the ordinary Magisterium, including the definitive confirmation or reaffirmation by a Pope that a teaching is required to safeguard and explain faithfully the deposit of faith.[21]

---

[21] See CCC 891–92; 2035; *The Code of Canon Law*, canon 750; and Catholics

Still, some Christians will cite the First Letter of St. John to argue that there is no need for Tradition or a Magisterium to understand Scripture—and thus all of God's saving truth:

> I write this to you about those who would deceive you; but the anointing which you received from him abides in you, and you have no need that any one should teach you; as his anointing teaches you about everything, and is true, and is no lie, just as it has taught you, abide in him. And now, little children, abide in him, so that when he appears we may have confidence and not shrink from him in shame at his coming (1 Jn. 2:26–28).

St. John is not saying that Christians are without need of any teachers to understand God's word, however. If that were so, Philip wouldn't have instructed the Ethiopian eunuch as he did. And, as one of the original Twelve Apostles, John understood the importance of apostolic authority, how that authority is handed to apostolic successors (as discussed in Chapter 1), and the value of other Apostolic Tradition, which various scriptural passages affirm.

Rather, John is telling his Christian audience that they are grounded in their faith *because* of apostolic preaching and teaching from him and other faithful teachers. Thus, they are in no need of teachers *who attempt to deceive them.* John does this in warning them about wayward Christian teachers who operate under the spirit of the antichrist, i.e., who deny that Jesus is the Christ (1 Jn. 2:18–28). So John reassures them as baptized Christians who are guided by the

---

United for the Faith (CUF) Faith Fact "The Infallibility of the Magisterium of the Catholic Church"; http://www.cuf.org/2002/11/pillar-and-bulwark-of-the-truth-the-infallibility-magisterium-of-the-catholic-church/.

Holy Spirit in their faith. He *doesn't* say they are in no need of being taught by *authentically faithful* Church leaders.

St. Paul affirms the need for Church leaders—including apostles and teachers—to maintain order and doctrinal purity (Eph. 4:11–14).

Furthermore, some teachings are not clear from Scripture alone, and thus we see additional need for a Magisterium and sacred Tradition. Through what is known as "development of doctrine," the Church more deeply grasps fundamental truths regarding faith or morals, which are either contained in the Church's deposit of faith or are needed to preserve, explain or observe those saving truths (see CCC 2035; 84; 890–91). For example, Jesus was understood to be God based on his own words (e.g., Jn. 8:58) and that of his apostles and other disciples (e.g., Jn. 1:1–3, 14). Yet, some called that doctrine into question.

Although the New Testament canon was not determined until the late 300s, books the Church deemed sacred were early on proclaimed at Mass, and read and preached about otherwise. St. Paul spoke often of "God our Father and the Lord Jesus Christ" (1 Cor. 1:3). Does that mean that only the Father is God and Jesus is the highest of all creatures but still a creature, as a man named Arius maintained? What about Jesus' own words regarding his Second Coming: "But of that day and hour no one knows, not even the angels of heaven, *nor the Son*, but the Father only" (Mt. 24:36, emphasis added).[22] Was Jesus telling us he had limited knowledge and therefore could not be God?

---

[22] In Matthew 24:36, Jesus engages in hyperbole, an overstatement to make the point that revealing such knowledge is not part of his earthly mission (see

Arius' movement continued, so in 325 the Church held a council in Nicaea, located in modern-day Turkey, to address the crisis. Appeals to *sola Scriptura* would not suffice, as Arius and his associates were not to be persuaded. *The Church* had to intervene, lest the faithful be led into grave error. The Council's teachings, approved by Pope St. Sylvester I, reaffirmed and dogmatically defined that Jesus is eternal God, and that he and the Father are truly one —each wholly possessing the same divine nature—and yet they are two distinct divine persons.[23] Similarly, the First Council of Constantinople in 381 removed any doubt that the Holy Spirit is a divine person, although one with the Father and the Son in the Holy Trinity.

Finally, without a Magisterium provided by God, how do Christians decide which books are in the New Testament canon? As then-budding Scripture scholar Scott Hahn journeyed toward the Catholic Church, his erudite mentors had to admit that, from a Protestant perspective, the best answer they could provide was, "We have no infallible authority but Scripture. . . . All we have is a fallible collection of

---

CCC 474). Jewish rabbis used hyperbole as a teaching device, and so did Jesus. Consider, for example, when Jesus says, "And call no man your father on earth, for you have one Father, who is in heaven" (Mt. 23:9). In colorfully affirming his heavenly Father's primacy, Jesus exhorts his followers to cultivate humility, not the pride that accompanies and fuels self-seeking status. He's not banning any other use of "father," as he himself calls mere human men "father" (e.g., Mt. 10:21, 35, 37), and St. Paul refers to himself as a spiritual father of the Corinthians (1 Cor. 4:15). See *The Ignatius Catholic Study Bible New Testament*, 52.

[23] See CCC 472–74 on the interplay between Jesus' divine personhood and his limited human nature. The Arian heresy persisted for a few hundred more years, but the Magisterium's teaching provided a light for the faithful amidst the heretical darkness.

infallible documents."[24] Yet, how can you know that your documents are infallible when you acknowledge that the collection process for those documents *was itself* fallible? *You can't.*

The reason any Christian can have confidence in the canon of Scripture is because the Catholic Church authoritatively compiled it, under the guidance of God. As Hahn came increasingly to see, Scripture doesn't claim to be an exclusive authority but rather points to a living authority outside of itself—a Magisterial authority—to faithfully interpret and safeguard the truth contained within its divinely inspired pages (see CCC 105–8). Hahn couldn't overcome that the Bible teaches, as St. Paul proclaims, that "the pillar and bulwark of the truth" is "the Church of the living God" (1 Tim. 3:15).[25]

The Catholic Church is indeed that Church. As Hahn says, "How many churches even claim to be the pillar and foundation of truth?"[26] Scripture testifies to the Church's rule of faith, as does unwritten Apostolic Tradition and 20 centuries of Church history. Jesus promised to be with his Church until the end of time here on earth (Mt. 28:20). Through the Magisterium's faithful interpretation and safeguarding of Scripture and Tradition—not to mention the celebration of the sacraments, particularly the Eucharist[27]—Jesus has been, is now and will be until he visibly returns at his Second Coming (see CCC 673–82).

---

[24] Scott and Kimberly Hahn, *Rome Sweet Home: Our Journey to Catholicism* (San Francisco: Ignatius Press, 1993), 73–74.

[25] Ibid., 53–54.

[26] Ibid., 54.

[27] See Chapter 4 on the Eucharist in particular and Chapter 6 on the sacraments in general.

3

"What Must I Do to Be Saved?"
(Acts 16:30; see Mt. 19:16)

Successfully Navigating the Highway to Heaven

How does Jesus save us?

Many books have been written on this question, but here we have only one relatively short chapter to distill an answer. All Christians agree that we can't save ourselves. A monk named Pelagius taught otherwise in the 400s, and the Catholic Church condemned his teaching as heretical. The sweep of Jesus' redemptive work begins with his becoming man at the Incarnation, so that we could become like God, "partakers of the divine nature" (2 Pet. 1:4; CCC 460). It continues into his earthly ministry and culminates with his one Sacrifice of Calvary[1] to atone for our sins, as Jesus suffers, dies, rises and ascends to the heavenly sanctuary so that we might one day reign with him in glory (CCC 1988; see 1 Cor. 15:42–45).

But does God predetermine who will go to heaven or hell before creating us, as John Calvin taught? Are we saved by faith alone, as Martin Luther first taught? Or is salvation a gift from God that we initially receive without any merit

---

[1] I prefer to use the phrase "Sacrifice *of* Calvary"—or "Offering *of* Calvary" —rather than "Sacrifice *on* Calvary", because the events of Jesus' one Sacrifice are not limited to his Passion—including the events leading up to his crucifixion—and Death *on* the Cross.

of our own, but which we need to appropriate more deeply —or reject—through our free-will choices, as the Catholic Church teaches?

Jesus points us toward the right answer in his encounter with the rich young man:

> And behold, one came up to him, saying, "Teacher, what good deed must I do, to have eternal life?" And he said to him, "Why do you ask me about what is good? One there is who is good. _If you would enter life, keep the commandments._" He said to him, "Which?" And Jesus said, "You shall not kill, You shall not commit adultery, You shall not steal, You shall not bear false witness, Honor your father and mother, and, You shall love your neighbor as yourself." The young man said to him, "All these I have observed; what do I still lack?" Jesus said to him, "_If you would be perfect,_ go, sell what you possess and give to the poor, and you will have treasure in heaven; and _come, follow me._" When the young man heard this he went away sorrowful; for he had great possessions.
>
> And Jesus said to his disciples, "Truly, I say to you, _it will be hard for a rich man to enter the kingdom of heaven._ Again I tell you, it is easier for a camel to go through the eye of a needle than for a rich man to enter the kingdom of God." When the disciples heard this they were greatly astonished, saying, "Who then can be saved?" But Jesus looked at them and said to them, "With men this is impossible, but with God all things are possible" (Mt. 19:16–26, emphases added).

Jesus doesn't tell the rich young man that God has already determined his eternal fate, in contrast to what you would expect if John Calvin were correct. And Jesus doesn't say that all the young man must do is simply believe, which differs from Martin Luther's "faith alone" position. Instead, Jesus tells the young man that his everyday choices _do_ make a difference regarding his salvation, and specifically notes keeping the Ten Commandments, the heart of the moral law that God revealed to Moses. He also conveys that the young man cannot make an idol of his possessions, allowing them to impede his allegiance to God.

Jesus' words to the rich young man are not exceptional comments that are out of sync with the usual thrust of his teaching; rather, they are typical. Our salvation undoubtedly *begins* with faith,[2] *but* it doesn't *end* there. Faith enables us to be engrafted into Christ *so that we can bear fruit for him and his kingdom*. Indeed, consider the famous Sermon on the Mount (Mt. 5—7), in which Jesus notes several times that our personal choices or works—and not simply our faith—will impact our eternal destiny for better or for worse, including:

> "For if you forgive men their trespasses, your heavenly Father also will forgive you; but if you do not forgive men their trespasses, neither will your Father forgive your trespasses" (Mt. 6:14–15).

> "Enter by the narrow gate; for the gate is wide and the way is easy, that leads to destruction, and those who enter by it are many. For the gate is narrow and the way is hard, that leads to life, and those who find it are few" (Mt. 7:13–14; see 5:20; 16:24–27).

> "Not every one who says to me, 'Lord, Lord,' shall enter the kingdom of heaven, but he who does the will of my Father who is in heaven. On that day many will say to me, 'Lord, Lord, did we not prophesy in your name, and cast out demons

---

[2] For one who becomes a member of Christ's Church as a baptized infant or young child, this would mean the faith of their parents on their behalf. That's similar to how the faith of parents sufficed for infant males who became members of ancient Israel via circumcision.

in your name, and do many mighty works in your name?'
And then will I declare to them, 'I never knew you; depart
from me, you evildoers'" (Mt. 7:21–23; see 25:31–46).

Consider these passages from St. Matthew's Gospel more
closely. God's forgiveness of us depends upon our forgiveness of others, and unforgiven sin means we are unclean
and unworthy of heaven (see Rev. 21:27). The road to
heaven is very difficult, whereas the road to hell is easy
(Mt. 7:13–14). And simply calling upon the name of Jesus
as Lord and Savior is insufficient for salvation (Mt. 7:21–
23).

In the Sermon on the Mount, Jesus teaches plainly that
salvation is not a one-time event, but a lifelong adventure.
Consequently, we can lose our salvation because of gravely
wrong actions for which we don't repent, as St. Paul affirms
(1 Cor. 6:9–10). These transgressions are known as mortal
sins, because they constitute a radical rejection of Jesus
in making someone and/or something an idol (see CCC
1854–64).

Competing Views on Original Sin
and the Remedy of Baptism

Despite Jesus' repeated and emphatic words, particularly in
the Gospel of Matthew, Luther and Calvin took exception
to the necessity of good works as a condition for salvation. All Christians believe that mankind was negatively
impacted by the sin of the first human couple, which is
called "original sin" (CCC 402–7). In their original "state
of holiness and justice," Adam and Eve shared in God's
divine life—"sanctifying grace"—as the Holy Trinity inti-

mately dwelled within them (CCC 375; 1997–2000). Original sin robs mankind thereafter of divine communion, requiring a Redeemer to restore our relationship with God and atone for all of our personal sins too.

While all Christians agree that Jesus is the Redeemer, they disagree on how original sin impacts human nature and therefore our ability to choose good and avoid evil. Catholics believe that original sin wounds our human nature, making choosing to do good more difficult because of a resulting inclination to do evil called "concupiscence" (CCC 405). Through the Sacrament of Baptism,[3] God forgives original and personal sins, and he gives us himself in sanctifying grace (CCC 1262), enabling us to live a life pleasing to him, one in which we strive to grow in holiness as his disciples. This baptismal grace, an undeserved divine gift, is known as "justification" (CCC 1266; 1987).

Jesus references Baptism when he tells Nicodemus we must be "born anew . . . of water and the Spirit" to enter the kingdom of God (Jn. 3:3–5), and confirms that Baptism is fundamental to making disciples of all nations (Mt. 28:18–20). Thus, on the Day of Pentecost, the birthday of the Church (CCC 1076), St. Peter tells his fellow Jews gathered to "repent, and be baptized every one of you in the name of Jesus Christ for the forgiveness of your sins; and you shall receive the gift of the Holy Spirit" (Acts 2:38). Likewise, when a Macedonian jailer asks what he must do

---

[3] While converts often become Catholics as adults, Baptism is the New Covenant analogue to circumcision in the Old (Col. 2:11–15; CCC 527), and so parents should have their children baptized; for to such, says Jesus, does the kingdom of God belong (see Mt. 19:13–15).

to be saved, St. Paul and Silas tell him to believe in Jesus and lead him to seal his new faith in the waters of Baptism (Acts 16:25–34); because, as Paul says elsewhere, Baptism is "the washing of regeneration and renewal in the Holy Spirit" (Tit. 3:5; see 1 Pet. 3:21; CCC 1215).

Baptism, also known as _initial_ justification, gives us a share in divine love or "righteousness," an infused "theological virtue"[4] which enables us to become like Jesus and do his will in a lovingly obedient way (CCC 1991). So Baptism restores man's communion with God and is the beginning of our salvation, the first step on a lifelong journey. In _ongoing_ justification or sanctification, we continue growing in the theological and human virtues, with Jesus as our model. This is not "works righteousness" or "salvation by works" as the Church's teaching is sometimes caricatured. Works alone, as Pelagius was reminded, can _never_ save. And works _apart from grace_ cannot even contribute to our salvation. Indeed, our good works only have "merit" —including graces for ourselves and others to grow in holiness and help attain eternal life—_because they are rooted in and aided by Christ's love_ (CCC 2006–16), so that we might persevere in God's grace instead of rejecting his gift of salvation. And if we are baptized after the age of reason, even the choice to receive Baptism is a good work, again aided by God's grace.

---

[4] The Church distinguishes between the three theological virtues—faith, hope and charity (i.e., love)—and human virtues that are acquired and developed through human effort (see CCC 1804–29), though aided, purified and elevated by God's grace. We benefit also from the gifts and fruits of the Holy Spirit (CCC 1830–32).

"What Must I Do to Be Saved?"

Luther agreed on the necessity of Baptism, that infants should be baptized and that one can lose their salvation by unrepented sin. But Luther had a radically different view of our sinful condition. Luther believed that original sin so injured man's nature that he is "totally depraved,"[5] incapable of doing any good regarding his salvation, even with God's help.[6]

---

[5] While John Calvin is more known for this doctrine, Luther espoused it also. See "Total Depravity" in Christian Apologetics and Research Ministry, *Dictionary of Theology*; https://carm.org/dictionary-total-depravity.

Romans 3:10–12 is a basic passage used to support the doctrine of total depravity. Paul says that "both Jews and Greeks are under the power of sin" (3:9) and then cites several passages from the Old Testament in 3:10–18 to make his point, including "[A]s it is written: 'None is righteous, no, not one; no one understands, no one seeks for God. All have turned aside, together they have gone wrong; no one does good, not even one'" (Rom. 3:10–12).

In isolation this passage and Romans 3:10–18 in general might seem to affirm the doctrine of total depravity. However, a closer analysis reveals more on 3:10–18:

> Six citations from the Old Testament confirm the charge that wickedness has flourished in Israel. The chain is made of links from Psalm 14:3, Psalm 5:9, Psalm 140:3, Psalm 10:7, Isaiah 59:7–8 and Psalm 36:1. Many of these passages distinguish between the righteous and the wicked, suggesting that Paul is not condemning every single Israelite without exception. His point is that sin has taken hold of the covenant people as it has the rest of the world. He is likewise showing that sin, which has spread throughout the body of mankind, has also spread through the body of every man who is prone to use his members as instruments of wickedness (6:13). All but one of these passages highlight a part of the body in this way (throat, tongues, lips in 3:13, mouth in 3:14, feet in 3:15, eyes in 3:18); (*The Ignatius Catholic Study Bible New Testament* [San Francisco: Ignatius Press, 2010], 261).

[6] Luther would still say that man has to trust in God to be saved, but that the actual process of saving is totally of God's doing. See further "Justify, Justification" in Christian Apologetics and Research Ministry, *Dictionary of Theology*; https://carm.org/dictionary-justification.

Consequently, despite the scriptural evidence to the contrary, Luther believed that Baptism neither imparts sanctifying grace nor purifies us of original sin and our personal sins. In *The Large Catechism*, Luther teaches that Baptism "is a laver of regeneration, as St. Paul also calls it" in Titus 3:5,[7] but this does not mean a restoration of the divine communion that Adam and Eve enjoyed. For Luther, regeneration means the removal of the *eternal punishment* of sin through the justifying faith associated with Baptism,[8] and thus it opens heaven to the justified. However, a justified person's human nature remains totally depraved for Luther, and original sin and an individual's personal sins are not blotted out; so communion with God is restored but in a lesser way than our first parents enjoyed. One needs to keep these distinctions in mind when Luther teaches that Baptism brings about the "forgiveness of sin."[9]

For Luther, justification is an *external* application of God's justice, a divine *declaration* that we are righteous, but without *inwardly*—or actually—removing original sin or our personal sins, and so without regenerating a person's soul through the infused power of the Holy Spirit. Instead, God the Father "imputes" to us—or credits us with—the perfect righteousness of Christ, won in his Sacrifice of Calvary.[10]

---

[7] Martin Luther, *The Large Catechism*, "Holy Baptism," no. 27; http://book ofconcord.org/lc-6-baptism.php.

[8] Ibid., nos. 41–46, 83.

[9] Ibid., nos. 41, 86. For Luther, concupiscence is evidence that man's regeneration is limited and thus original sin remains, that sanctifying grace is thus not restored, and that a person is not truly purified of their personal sins as well. So man ironically remains in his sins even though the eternal punishment associated with those sins is removed through justifying faith.

[10] As Dr. Timothy George, the longtime dean of Beeson Divinity School at

So justification for Luther is a one-time event only, because Christ's divine acts admit of no improvement, and Luther bases his doctrine on his reading of St. Paul's words in Romans 5:18: "Then as one man's trespass [Adam's original sin] led to condemnation for all men, so one man's act of righteousness[11] leads to acquittal and life for all men."[12]

Consequently, Luther preached that man is *simul justus et peccator*, that we are justified in God's eyes and yet simultaneously sinful, as if God were clothing us in a white blanket of righteousness while turning away his eyes from the darkness of our sins, instead of actually blotting them out.[13]

Samford University, writes, "According to the medieval understanding of justification, which was derived from Augustine, a person gradually receives divine grace, eventually healing sin's wounds. But in his mature doctrine of justification, Luther abandoned the medical image of *impartation* for the legal language of *imputation*: God accepts Christ's righteousness, which is alien to our nature, as our own. Though God does not actually remove our sins—we are at the same time righteous and sinful (*simul justus et peccator*)—he no longer counts them against us"; (George, "Dr. Luther's Theology," *Christian History*, Issue 34, 1992, emphases original); https://www.christianhistoryinstitute.org/magazine/article/dr-luthers-theology/.

[11] In saying "act of righteousness," Paul refers to Christ's collective Sacrifice of Calvary, i.e., his Passion, Death, Resurrection and Ascension.

[12] Again, see "Justify, Justification" in Christian Apologetics and Research Ministry, *Dictionary of Theology*; https://carm.org/dictionary-justification.

[13] See, e.g., *Luther's Works*, Vol. 34, 178 and 184. As cited in Dave Armstrong, "Luther's 'Snow-Covered Dunghill' (Myth?)"; http://www.patheos.com/blogs/davearmstrong/2016/04/luthers-snow-covered-dunghill-myth.html.

More recently, in 2001, the Catholic Church and the Lutheran World Federation signed a *Joint Declaration on the Doctrine of Justification*, with a Catholic annex to clarify a number of doctrinal points on which the Church differs from that expressed in the *Joint Declaration*. Both the *Joint Declaration* (JD) and the "Official Common Statement" (OCS) state that Catholics and Lutherans have reached "a consensus on basic truths of the doctrine of justification" (JD 5; OCS 1). This is the heart of the consensus—"Together we confess: By grace alone,

Because Luther argued that man is not actually purified of sin or spiritually empowered through Baptism, he taught in his Augsburg Confession of 1530 that "our works cannot reconcile us to God or merit remission of sins and grace and justification. This we obtain only by faith, when we believe that we are received into grace on account of Christ."[14]

Sola fide, or justification "by faith alone,"[15] became Luther's greatest theological legacy, and he rooted it in his reading of Romans 3:28, in which Paul says, "For we hold that a man is justified by faith apart from works of the law." Luther added "alone" in his translation of Paul's epistle, as in "faith alone," convinced that this was the apostle's meaning. As a means to rebut or explain away Jesus' words on the salvific importance of human choices, Luther drove a wedge between "Law" and "Gospel," based on his understanding of "works of the law" in Romans 3 and Galatians 2—3. For Luther, all teaching about works falls on the side of Law, which is ultimately a counterfeit

in faith in Christ's saving work and not because of any merit on our part, we are accepted by God and receive the Holy Spirit, who renews our hearts while equipping and calling us to good works" (JD 15; Catholic "Annex to the OCS," 2). Not all Lutheran groups signed, including the more conservative Missouri Synod Lutherans, because the renewal of man's hearts implies a real inner transformation and not simply a declaration of righteousness. For more, see Thomas J. Nash and Philip C. L. Gray, Catholics United for the Faith (CUF), "Not A Full Agreement: A Commentary on the *Joint Declaration on the Doctrine of Justification*"; http://www.catholicculture.org/news/features/index.cfm?recnum=20719.

[14] Martin Luther, *The Augsburg Confession*, Article XX ("Of Good Works"), 9. As cited in Fr. John Hardon, S.J., *Religions of the World, Vol. Two* (Garden City, NY: Image Books, 1968), 164.

[15] Though he differed strongly with Luther on the Eucharist (see Chapter 4), Ulrich Zwingli agreed with Luther that salvation comes by faith alone ("Zwingli's Sixty-Seven Articles," XV–XVI); https://www.christianhistoryinstitute.org/study/module/zwinglis-sixty-seven-articles/.

way of salvation, vs. the genuine and liberating Gospel attained "by faith alone."

This Law/Gospel dichotomy is seen clearly in Luther's comments on the Letter of James, notes Fr. Georges Florovsky, a twentieth-century Russian Orthodox theologian who taught at both Harvard and Princeton. Luther included James in his 1522 German New Testament, Fr. Florovsky says, but he described it as an "epistle of straw" in his preface to the letter because it has "no evangelical merit to it." He rejected James theologically, Luther explained in his preface,

> because it gives righteousness to works in outright contradiction to Paul and all other Scriptures . . . [and] because, while undertaking to teach Christian people, it does not once mention the passion, the resurrection, the Spirit of Christ; it names Christ twice, but teaches nothing about him; it calls the law a law of liberty, while Paul calls it a law of bondage, of wrath, of death and of sin.[16]

Justification by faith alone "is at the heart of the Protestant rejection of Catholicism," says Dr. David Anders. Luther, Anders adds, "called it 'the article on which the Church stands or falls.' Luther once said that if the Pope would only teach justification by faith, he would kiss the Pope's feet and carry him in his hands. One cannot overestimate how important this doctrine is to traditional Protestantism."[17]

---

[16] Luther, preface to the Letter of James. As cited in Fr. Georges Florovsky, "The Epistle of James and Luther's Evaluation," *The Byzantine Ascetic and Spiritual Fathers*; http://www.holytrinitymission.org/books/english/fathers_florovsky_4.htm#_Toc27729548.

[17] A. David Anders, Ph.D., "Protestants Becoming Catholic: Justification By Faith Alone"; http://calvin2catholic.com/?p=362. See also Anders, "A

Distinguishing Good Works from "Works of the Law"

A closer look at St. Paul's epistles, however, shows Paul's agreement with what Jesus teaches about good works in the Gospel. Paul was not brushing aside all good works; rather, he teaches that "works of the law,"[18] i.e., primarily the ritual and liturgical commandments which Moses prescribed for _Old Covenant_ life, cannot make a man righteous before God, because they are performed "apart from the grace of Christ."[19] However, for persons "already established in grace"[20] _as New Covenant disciples of Christ_, Paul teaches something quite different regarding their living out the timeless moral law grounded in the Ten Commandments: "For it is not the hearers of the law who are righteous before God, but the doers of the law who will be justified" (Rom. 2:13–15; see Jas. 1:22–25).

Such a reading of St. Paul is consistent with the teaching of St. James, who writes:

> What does it profit, my brethren, if a man says he has faith but has not works? Can his faith save him? If a brother or sister is ill-clad and in lack of daily food, and one of you says to them, "Go in peace, be warmed and filled," without giving them the things needed for the body, what does it profit? So faith by itself, if it has no works, is dead.
>
> But some one will say, "You have faith and I have works." Show me your faith apart from your works, and I by my works

---

Protestant Historian Discovers the Catholic Church"; http://chnetwork.org/story/a-protestant-historian-discovers-the-catholic-church-conversion-story-of-a-david-anders-ph-d/.

[18] See "The Works of the Law," _The Ignatius Catholic Study Bible New Testament_, 335.

[19] "Faith and Works," _The Ignatius Catholic Study Bible New Testament_ 443.

[20] Ibid.

will show you my faith. You believe that God is one; you do well. Even the demons believe—and shudder. Do you want to be shown, you foolish fellow, that faith apart from works is barren? Was not Abraham our father justified by works, when he offered his son Isaac upon the altar? You see that faith was active along with his works, and faith was completed by works, and the Scripture was fulfilled which says, "Abraham believed God, and it was reckoned to him as righteousness"; and he was called the friend of God. *You see that a man is justified by works and not by faith alone.* And in the same way was not also Rahab the harlot justified by works when she received the messengers and sent them out another way? For as the body apart from the spirit is dead, so faith apart from works is dead (Jas. 2:14–26, emphasis added).

In Matthew 12, consistent with Sts. Paul and James, Jesus makes unmistakably clear that our words and deeds *done in Christ* justify and therefore positively impact our salvation, whereas sinful actions do the opposite:

"The good man out of his good treasure brings forth good, and the evil man out of his evil treasure brings forth evil. I tell you, on the day of judgment men will render account for every careless word they utter; *for by your words you will be justified, and by your words you will be condemned*" (Mt. 12:35–37, emphasis added).

The same Greek word for "justification" that St. Paul uses to describe justification by faith in Romans 3:28—*dikaióō*—is the same word that St. Matthew (Mt. 12:37), St. Paul (Rom. 2:13) and St. James (Jas. 2:24) all use to describe justification by works regarding our moral conduct in living out the New Covenant.[21]

---

[21] Spiros Zodhiates, ed., *The Hebrew-Greek Key Study Bible*–New American Standard Bible version (Chattanooga, TN: AMG Publishers), 1490, 1279, 1487, 1639; and p. 23, no. 1344 of the "Greek Dictionary of the New Testament"

One should at least credit Luther with not attempting to twist the plain theological meaning of St. James' doctrinal content. Apparently, he couldn't bring himself to do the same with Jesus' similar words in the Gospels—again, using his reading of St. Paul as a wedge. Luther dropped his preface to James in subsequent editions of his Bible, but he never ceased to maintain the doctrinal outlook it expresses.

Projecting Personal Problems onto St. Paul:
Luther's Struggle with Scrupulosity

Luther suffered from scrupulosity, an obsessive concern with personal failings and an accompanying great difficulty to accept forgiveness, especially from God. So Luther struggled with a tortured conscience and an acute sense of inadequacy in the spiritual life, which robbed him of the peace that God wants his children to have. For Luther, no such peace was possible apart from an absolute certainty of salvation despite his personal failings. Luther's fundamental "by faith alone" justification doctrine developed in the process of dealing with his scrupulosity.[22]

---

appendix. Zodhiates makes the same mistake as Luther in conflating New Covenant (NC) good works with Old Covenant (OC) "works of the law" in referring the reader of James 2 (NC good works) to his analysis of Galatians 2:16 (OC works of the law) on 1552. See also the _Blue Letter Bible's_ treatment of _dikaióō_ at https://www.blueletterbible.org/lang/lexicon/lexicon.cfm?t=kjv&strongs=g1344.

[22] That Luther suffered from scrupulosity, at one time at least, is shared by both Protestant and Catholic scholars, although those in agreement with Luther would argue that his "faith alone" teaching was a genuine blessing in helping him remedy this psychological malady, whereas Catholic scholars would argue

So also did Luther's view that man has an "enslaved will," which exceeded the views of other Reformers like Calvin, who believed a person could do good deeds that positively impact their lives and the lives of others on earth, though Calvin attributed the good works to God. In *De Servo Arbitrio* ("On The Enslaved Will")—which along with his *Large Catechism* Luther said were his only significant works in his extensive writings—Luther presents God and the devil as competitors who fight to control man's actions: "The human will stands like a saddle horse between the two. If God mounts into the saddle, man wills and goes forward as God wills. . . . But if the devil is the horseman, then man wills and acts as the devil wills. He has no power to run to one or the other of the two riders and offer himself to him, but the riders fight to obtain possession of the animal."[23]

In saying that God and the devil "fight to obtain possession of the animal," Luther doesn't seem to grasp that his analogy blasphemes God, as if the devil could actually prevail over the Lord in a dualistic showdown. Not only does Luther give the devil undue credit here as a worthy competitor for his creator, he also presents a debased view of man—as a mere puppet or beast caught in a temporal tug-of-war between Satan and the Savior. For Luther, when God is "in the saddle," man can perform works of sanctification, whereby the Holy Spirit makes us more like

---

that it was a seriously erroneous doctrinal conclusion that helped him to deal with his scrupulosity better.

[23] *De Servo Arbitrio*, sect. 25. As cited in "Luther's Enduring Legacy," E. Michael Jones, *Degenerate Moderns: Modernity as Rationalized Sexual Misbehavior* (San Francisco: Ignatius Press, 1993) 237.

Christ in all we think, desire and choose.[24] But if the devil prevailed, man inevitably chose wrongly.

Building on the work of various scholars, Dr. E. Michael Jones argues that Luther not only suffered from scrupulosity but a genuinely guilty conscience. In examining Luther's German writings and those of Luther's friends regarding the Reformer's life, Jones concludes that Luther's "faith alone" and "enslaved will" doctrines enabled the German theologian to console his conscience:

> With free will goes culpability. In order to obliterate his culpability for the death of the peasants, for the breaking of solemn vows, for the sins of the flesh, for the fracturing of the unity of Christendom,[25] Luther must obliterate free will. For if in fact the will is free, he would have to answer for what he had done before God. Luther's doctrine of the enslaved will flows directly from his troubled conscience. The doctrine of the enslaved will that lies at the heart of the Lutheran ideology is at heart the admission of a man who struggled against evil and then failed, and then tried to rationalize the failure by claiming that there was no struggle. "I have often attempted to become good," Luther said in a sermon he gave in 1524, "however, the more I struggle, the less I succeed. Behold then, what free will is."[26]

An increasing number of Protestant scholars, Anders reports, recognize that Luther profoundly misread the writings of St. Paul because he projected his personal struggles

---

[24] See further "Sanctify, Sanctification" in Christian Apologetics and Research Ministry, _Dictionary of Theology_; https://carm.org/dictionary-sanctification.

[25] "The unity of Christendom" here refers to once-Catholic Europe, not the divine mark of unity which the Church can never lose (see CCC 811–16).

[26] "Luther's Enduring Legacy" in Jones, _Degenerate Moderns_, 249.

onto Paul, instead of viewing the apostle as he really was: "a self-assured Pharisaical Jew of the first century."[27] Anders says reading St. Paul in context has led to a number of conversions to Catholicism over the last several decades:

> Protestant students and scholars are becoming more willing to criticize their own traditions and to reexamine the teaching of Scripture. When they do this, they find that Luther's doctrine is very difficult to square with the Bible. It takes a lot of mental gymnastics to squeeze Luther through texts like Romans 2:13, James 2:24, 1 John 2:4, or Matthew 19:17.[28]

One might understandably wonder that if Luther believed man's will is enslaved, how could the Reformer simultaneously believe that a person could fall away from justifying faith and lose their salvation? Such a serious break with God would necessarily entail the *free* rejection of God in a grave matter, what Catholics would describe as mortal sin (see CCC 1855–61). Luther also distinguished between mortal and venial sins in his early days as a Reformer, then abandoned the distinction altogether, though he still used the term "mortal sin" in giving "clear advice," as one Lutheran scholar says, "to confess only known mortal sins that trouble the conscience in full awareness that even good deeds, without God's mercy, are only deadly deeds."[29]

Despite believing in the enslaved will, and that "free will,

---

[27] Anders, "Protestants Becoming Catholic: Justification By Faith Alone"; http://calvin2catholic.com/?p=362.

[28] Ibid.

[29] Dr. Ľubomír Batka, "Martin Luther's Teaching on Sin," *Oxford Research Encyclopedia of Religion*, December 2016; http://religion.oxfordre.com/view/10.1093/acrefore/9780199340378.001.0001/acrefore-9780199340378-e-373.

after the fall, exists in name only,"[30] Luther also taught in _The Heidelberg Disputation_ of 1518 that "free will, after the fall, has power to do good only in a passive capacity, but it can always do evil in an active capacity."[31] Seven years later in _De Servo Arbitrio_, as noted, Luther seems less confident about man's free will do evil. Luther was not always consistent in his doctrinal pronouncements, charitably stated. In any event, if man's will were truly enslaved, it would seem rather difficult to speak of crediting a person for any contribution to their justifying faith or penalizing them for any serious transgression. On the other hand, as we have seen, Jesus teaches that man's will, despite the fall, is free and that our free choices undoubtedly play a key role in our accepting or rejecting God's gift of salvation. St. Paul and St. James echo the importance of justifying good works in Christ, and they add that we can also be justly excluded from heaven through freely committed and unrepented mortal sins (Gal. 5:16–21; Jas. 5:19–20).

Double Predestination:
Calvin's "Dreadful Decree" on Salvation

Calvin agreed with Luther that, because of the total depravity of man's soul which Baptism could not rectify, good works cannot contribute to our salvation. And yet, like Luther, Calvin also believed in the necessity of Baptism, even for infants, since especially for Calvin helpless infants

---

[30] Luther, _The Heidelberg Disputation_, no. 13; http://bookofconcord.org/heidelberg.php.

[31] Ibid., no. 14.

illustrate beautifully that the justification which comes by Baptism is a pure gift of God.[32] But Calvin ultimately went much further than Luther regarding man's salvation. Based on his readings of passages in Matthew 15 and Romans 9, Calvin believed that God in his divine sovereignty—i.e., in his supreme power over life and death—predestines some to heaven (the elect) and others to hell (the reprobate). Consequently, for Calvin, there is nothing a person can really do to change their eternal destiny, nor can anyone presume to question why God wills some to be saved and others to be damned irrespective of their choices. This doctrine is known as "double predestination."[33]

Calvin's doctrine on salvation can be summed up in the acronym TULIP: Total depravity of man resultant from original sin; Unconditional election of man, affirming that some will undoubtedly be saved; Limited atonement, for God does not will all to be saved; Irresistible grace, for the elect will not be able to resist God's saving grace, and Perseverance of the saints, reaffirming that those whom God has elected for salvation will indeed be saved.[34]

Catholic apologist James Akin says that one must not oversimplify Calvin's position on salvation:

> Calvinists are sometimes wrongly criticized as teaching that a person may as well be unconcerned about his salvation since he is already either among the elect or the reprobate. According to Calvin, it would be a mistake for a person to

---

[32] I. John Hesselink, *On Being Reformed: Distinctive Characteristics and Common Misunderstandings* (Ann Arbor, MI: Servant Books, 1983), 95–96.

[33] Zwingli also believed in a variation on double predestination.

[34] See James Akin, *The Salvation Controversy* (San Diego: Catholic Answers, 2001), 72–87.

say, "Well, if God chooses me I'll be saved; if he doesn't, I won't. So I can sit back and do nothing." Calvinists rightly point out that a person who says this until his death shows that he was not one of the elect because he never did the things, such as repenting and trusting God, that are necessary for salvation.[35]

Still, for Calvin, the fact remains that God in his sovereignty predetermines that he will save some and reprobate others, and so his plan will ultimately play out accordingly in their respective lives. As noted, Calvin believed that such reprobated men could perform noble achievements on earth in the fields of math, medicine, literature, etc., but only because of God.[36] And their terrestrial accomplishments would ultimately be in vain, given their divinely predetermined eternal destiny.

Calvin based his view, in part, on his reading of Jesus' words in Matthew 15:

> And he called the people to him and said to them, "Hear and understand: not what goes into the mouth defiles a man, but what comes out of the mouth, this defiles a man." Then the disciples came and said to him, "Do you know that the Pharisees were offended when they heard this saying?" He answered, *"Every plant which my heavenly Father has not planted will be rooted up.* Let them alone; they are blind guides. And if a blind man leads a blind man, both will fall into a pit" (Mt. 15:10–14, emphasis added).

---

[35] Ibid., 73.

[36] John Calvin, *The Institutes of the Christian Religion*, Henry Beveridge, trans., bk. 2, ch. 2, sects. 14–17; https://www.ccel.org/ccel/calvin/institutes.iv.iii.html. To access *The Institutes* more generally, see https://www.ccel.org/ccel/calvin/institutes.toc.html.

Did Jesus and St. Paul Teach Divine Reprobation?

Regarding Matthew 15:13, Calvin says, "They are plainly told that all whom the heavenly Father has not been pleased to plant as sacred trees in his garden, are doomed and devoted to destruction. If they deny that this is a sign of reprobation, there is nothing, however clear, that can be proved to them."[37] Calvin's narrow reading of this isolated verse regarding Jesus' words about the Pharisees presumes that each man has no say in whether he takes root with the Father. In addition Calvin overlooks—*within this same passage from Matthew 15, no less*—that Jesus implies that a man will be judged, in part, by what he says and does. In the process Jesus, like St. Paul, sharply distinguishes between *violations of Old Covenant works of the law that don't defile*, e.g., eating with unwashed hands, and *violations of the timeless moral law which do defile*, e.g., murder and adultery. And so what Calvin cited from Matthew 15 looks much different in full context:

> And he called the people to him and said to them, "Hear and understand: not what goes into the mouth defiles a man, but what comes out of the mouth, this defiles a man." Then the disciples came and said to him, "Do you know that the Pharisees were offended when they heard this saying?" He answered, "Every plant which my heavenly Father has not planted will be rooted up. Let them alone; they are blind guides. And if a blind man leads a blind man, both will fall into a pit." But Peter said to him, "Explain the parable to us." And he said, *"Are you also still without understanding? Do you not*

---

[37] Ibid., bk. 3, ch. 23, sect. 1; https://www.ccel.org/ccel/calvin/institutes.v.xxiv .html.

see that whatever goes into the mouth passes into the stomach, and so passes on? But what comes out of the mouth proceeds from the heart, and this defiles a man. For out of the heart come evil thoughts, murder, adultery, fornication, theft, false witness, slander. These are what defile a man; but to eat with unwashed hands does not defile a man" (Mt. 15:10–20, emphasis added).

Jesus tells us that the Father sent him to save the world, that whoever _believes_ in him will be saved and those who _do not_ believe won't be saved (Jn. 3:16–18). So we are _free_ to accept or reject Jesus, which, as discussed earlier, Jesus also makes clear in the Sermon on the Mount, his words to the rich young man, etc.

Indeed, Jesus _never_ teaches that some men are beyond salvation, including the Pharisees that he mentions in Matthew 15, the _same men_ who helped to engineer Jesus' death. Regarding these men, as well as the chief priests and others who collaborated in his crucifixion, Jesus says something quite different: "Father, _forgive them_; for they know not what they do" (Lk. 23:34, emphasis added). Jesus' words make no sense if Calvin's reading of Matthew 15 is true. But they make much sense if man has a free will, and that even those who actively work against God and his kingdom can subsequently be planted and reconciled to him.

Calvin also cited St. Paul's words in Romans 9 to support his doctrine of the reprobate:

But if they will still murmur, let us in the soberness of faith rest contented with the admonition of Paul, that it can be no ground of complaint that God, _"willing to show his wrath, and to make his power known, endured with much long-suffering the_ *vessels of wrath fitted for destruction*: and that he might make known the riches of his glory on the vessels of mercy, which he had afore prepared unto glory" (Rom. 9:22–23, emphasis added).[38]

Such an interpretation does not fit with what Paul has written elsewhere, in particular to St. Timothy, when he says that God "desires *all* men to be saved and come to the knowledge of the truth" (1 Tim. 2:4, emphasis added; see 4:10). Paul makes no exception for the reprobate here; he speaks categorically. Similarly, St. Peter confirms that "God is forbearing toward you, not wishing that *any* should perish, but that *all* should reach repentance" (2 Pet. 3:9, emphases added; see CCC 1037).

Either St. Paul is contradicting himself under the inspiration of the Holy Spirit, and St. Peter and St. John (see 1 Jn. 2:2) are similarly misguided, or Romans 9:22–23 does not mean what Calvin thought it meant. Regarding the crucial phrase in Romans 9:22—"made [fitted] for destruction"— *The Ignatius Catholic Study Bible New Testament* provides insight:

> The Greek can mean that the vessels of wrath have prepared themselves for doom by rejecting the Gospel. Paul is not saying that God has predestined the unbelievers of Israel for damnation; otherwise he would not be praying (10:1) and working (11:14) for their salvation (CCC 1037).[39]

---

[38] Ibid.

[39] *The Ignatius Catholic Study Bible New Testament*, 270.

Double Predestination:
A Doctrine Not Worthy of God

Only by isolating a couple of statements by Jesus and St. Paul, and then distorting them in relation to what Jesus and Paul have taught at length elsewhere, can Calvin come to his depressing doctrine of double predestination. This doctrine, Calvin said, "I admit, is, dreadful; and yet it is impossible to deny that God foreknew what the end of man was to be before he made him, and foreknew, because he had so ordained by his decree."[40]

Calvin seems to say that because God omnisciently knows all choices before we make them, he must therefore have ordained them to occur. The whole of human history is indeed *present* to God, because God, who is all-powerful, cannot be limited by the time and space he creates, as well as the human persons who operate within that created realm. As a result, God knows our choices *in our choosing them*, because he does not have to wait for them to unfold in the actual living of our lives to know the outcome. But God's *knowing* how we'll choose doesn't mean that he *predetermines* how we'll choose, as if human history is a divine puppet show in which only God gets to pull the strings.[41] Rather, given man's divine gift of free will that both Jesus and St. Paul affirm, God allows us to cooperate in our salvation, to accept or reject that most precious gift.

---

[40] Calvin, *The Institutes of the Christian Religion*, bk. 3, ch. 23, sect. 7. https://www.ccel.org/ccel/calvin/institutes.v.xxiv.html.

[41] And if somehow we had a measure of free will on earth but couldn't impact our eternal salvation, that would be of little consolation.

More to the point, in arguing for God's sovereignty in the way he does, Calvin also unwittingly blasphemes God by presenting him as a capricious tyrant who is responsible for the greatest of evils: consigning men to hell without giving them any real opportunity to accept or reject him. Calvin defends his position by saying we have no right to question God on this matter, but what his critics are questioning is actually Calvin's concept of God's goodness. Double predestination makes God, not the godless sinner, responsible for human sin. I am reminded of the movie "The Wizard of Oz," in which Dorothy and her friends are told by a great and menacing wizard to "pay no attention to that man behind the curtain." And yet, when Dorothy and her friends do pay attention, they realize the wizard is not so great, but only the creation and projection of a mere man.[42]

The same is true regarding Calvin's belief about God on the issue of double predestination. As Calvin presents him, he may be a god, but he is not the God of the Scriptures, who is loving, merciful, etc. Instead, in deliberately reprobating many to hell, God becomes guilty of far worse sins than any mere human person could commit in their lifetime, because God is supposed to personify perfect love and thus be immune to committing sin, whereas man operates with a fallen nature and is thus vulnerable to transgressing. In addition, the doctrine of reprobation presents God as an unjust dictator and is antithetical to any standard of true love. In that light, Calvin's standard for God's love

---

[42] For the related movie clip, see https://www.youtube.com/watch?v=NZR64E F3OpA.

and concern for his creatures falls woefully short of mere human mothers and fathers who desperately desire *all* of their children to attain heaven. If finite creatures made in God's image and likeness have such loving concern for their children, how much more should we expect from the infinite, eternal God?

John Wesley, an Anglican cleric and co-founder of Methodism in the 1700s, also strongly condemned the doctrine of double predestination, which Fr. John Hardon, S.J., refers to as "predestinarianism" in summarizing Wesley's position:

> Wesley's main concern was with the salvation of all men. He was convinced that Christ came to seek and save that which was lost, and the Church is commissioned to preach the Gospel of redemption. But if predestinarianism is true, Christ's advent was in vain, because there is no need (or possibility) of saving the unsavable. Multitudes are beyond the love of God and nothing can be done to help them. He considered this a repudiation of the central truth of Christianity.[43]

Seeking Salvation:
Going God's Way

As we have seen, though, God the Father truly desires the salvation of the world—*the whole world*. That's why he sent his Son to save us. Whether the whole world accepts his

---

[43] Fr. Hardon, *Religions of the World, Vol. Two*, 191. Indeed, if double predestination were true, one would expect Jesus to qualify his many exhortations regarding striving for holiness and salvation as *not* applying to the reprobate, for whom eternal damnation would be a foregone conclusion. But Jesus *doesn't*, whether in the Sermon on the Mount or elsewhere, conveying like Sts. Peter and Paul that God desires to save *all*.

gift of salvation is another matter. But that man has a free will to accept or reject that gift is something that Jesus and Sts. Peter, Paul, James, etc., are of *one* mind—*we do.*

And though they hail Luther and Calvin as real Reformers of God's Church, many Protestant Christians have departed from the early Reformers on key issues. Jacob Arminius—from whom we get the name "Arminians"—couldn't accept Calvin's "Dreadful Decree," and so logically opted to teach that God could foreknow our destiny without predetermining it. And many other Christians have subsequently departed from Luther[44] and Calvin on the necessity of Baptism for salvation—strongly opposing infant Baptism, in particular—and have instead espoused "believer's baptism," arguing that one must *personally* accept Jesus as their personal Lord and Savior to be saved (see Rom. 10:9–10). Baptism comes afterward as a mere ordinance done out of obedience, not because it has any power to save. This is a classic doctrine embraced by many Protestants today, including many Baptists.

Many modern Protestants also believe in "once saved/always saved," that a man cannot lose his salvation once he accepts Jesus, and here they depart from Luther who believed that believers could "backslide" and fall out of favor with God through loss of faith. On the other hand, there are many Protestants, including various Evangelicals, who espouse the reality of backsliding, a Protestant term for losing the fervor of faith and drifting back into a life of sin.

---

[44] Zwingli also believed in Infant Baptism, but had a lower theological view of it than Luther and Calvin.

In summary, as with the rule of faith, so also we see with the matter of salvation. Beginning with Luther and Calvin, Protestant Christians have ironically replaced sacred Tradition with their own "development of doctrine"[45] and thus manmade religious traditions, and their spiritual descendants have developed them further, often in ways that contradict Luther and Calvin—*even on matters as important as how we are saved.* The Protestant Reformation and its centuries-long aftermath illustrate these sad realities. And this despite all concerned parties vowing to adhere strictly to "the Bible alone" in advancing their respective, though differing, doctrines.

The Catholic Church exists to teach fully and faithfully Christ's saving truth, including that which the Holy Spirit guided the Apostles to know after Jesus' Ascension (see CCC 76; 84). We want to be fully going God's way on the road to salvation, and not a way that falls short in one significant way or another. The Catholic Church serves as man's divinely provided and protected sure guide to navigate our journey home to heaven.

Jesus earnestly desires to welcome everyone into his divine family.[46] Having concluded that salvation is available

---

[45] As discussed in Chapter 2, in authentic development of doctrine the Church more deeply grasps fundamental truths regarding faith or morals, which are either contained in the Church's deposit of faith or are needed to preserve, explain or observe those saving truths (see CCC 2035; 84; 890–91). Authentic development necessarily precludes doctrinal contradictions. See also Vatican II, *Dei Verbum* (DV), 8–10.

[46] Regarding the salvation of non-Catholics, see footnote 17 in the Introduction.

to all through our free response to God, beginning in Baptism, we will explore in subsequent chapters the various means by which God helps us in that cooperative venture, beginning with the Eucharist or Sacrifice of the Mass, which Protestants generally refer to as "the Lord's Supper." In all these means, we can know that Jesus fulfills his promise that he will be with us in his Church until he returns again at his Second Coming (see Mt. 28:20; CCC 671–79).

4

"Do This in Memory of Me"
(Luke 22:19)

The Fundamental Importance of the
Sacrifice of the Eucharist (Mass)/Lord's Supper

At the Last Supper, when Jesus tells his apostles, "Take, eat; this is my body" (Mt. 26:26), and "Do this in remembrance[1] of me" (Lk. 22:19), what does he mean? From the time of the Reformation to the present, the meaning of the Lord's Supper/Sacrifice of the Mass has been one of the most controversial issues dividing Catholic and Protestant Christians. And that's understandable, given the Catholic Church teaches that the Liturgy of the Eucharist[2] or Mass[3] is "the source and summit of the Christian life,"[4] which is one of various fundamental teachings on which Catholics and Orthodox Christians enjoy unity (CCC 1399).[5]

---

[1] In English Masses of the Latin/Roman Rite, the word is translated as "memory."

[2] The word "Eucharist" comes from the Greek "*Eucharistia*," meaning "thanksgiving" or "giving thanks."

[3] There are various titles signifying the same rich reality of the Eucharistic Sacrifice. See CCC 1328–32.

[4] CCC 1324, citing Vatican II, *Lumen Gentium* (LG), 11.

[5] Though the Orthodox are not in full communion with the Catholic Church, these Eastern Churches affirm and celebrate validly all seven sacraments, which

In short, the Church makes deeply profound theological claims about the Mass in her teaching, including:

- The liturgy of the Eucharist makes present anew the one and only Sacrifice of Jesus Christ, the divine Bridegroom who laid down his life to redeem us, his mystical bride, the Church.[6]

- Because Jesus' one Sacrifice *culminated in everlasting glory in the heavenly sanctuary* at his Ascension (see Heb. 9:11–14, 23–24), the Body and Blood of Jesus that is present in the Sacrament of the Eucharist is his resurrected and glorified Body, not his mortal, suffering body. So Jesus does not suffer and die anew at each Mass,[7] as the Eucharistic Sacrifice has sometimes been caricatured. Rather, his completed, glorified and everlasting Sacrifice is made present in an "unbloody manner,"[8] i.e., without the shedding anew of his blood.

- The presence of Jesus' Body and Blood is real, yet concealed behind the sensible attributes or properties of bread and wine. The Church refers to the Eucharist as

---

means their bishops have valid apostolic succession and their priesthood in general is valid as well (CCC 1399). One obstacle to full reunion between Catholics and the Orthodox, however, is the Orthodox practice of allowing divorce and remarriage within their churches without requiring either an annulment or a dissolution for prospective spouses in need of them.

[6] See Eph. 5:21–33. For more on the wondrous truth of Jesus' love for us, see Brant Pitre, *Jesus the Bridegroom: The Greatest Love Story Ever Told* (New York: Image, 2014).

[7] Jesus suffered and died once for all on Good Friday (Heb. 7:27; 9:28).

[8] CCC 1367; 1369.

the "Real Presence" (see CCC 1378–79), because Jesus is present in his "body and blood" and "soul and divinity": "Christ, God and man, makes himself wholly and entirely present" (CCC 1374; see 1373; 1413).[9]

So Catholics believe that the Mass "re-presents"—or makes present anew—Christ's *one* Sacrifice of Calvary[10] (CCC 1366). That is, the substance or the essence of the bread and wine are miraculously changed through a process called "transubstantiation" (see CCC 1376–77), while the properties or "accidents" of bread and wine, i.e., the aspects discernible by our human senses—sight, taste, touch/feel, hear, and smell—remain.[11]

Jesus doesn't die anew, because Scripture makes clear he triumphed over sin and death, perfecting his humanity and thereby rendering it immortal. Thus, Jesus holds his priesthood *permanently* and so lives to make intercession for us *always* (Heb. 7:23–25), because he rose from

---

[9] The celebration or Sacrifice of the Eucharist/Mass as a whole is distinguished from the Eucharist, or consecrated Host, which the Catholic faithful receive at Mass. Because Jesus' Real Presence endures, the faithful adore their Eucharistic Lord both at Mass and outside of it (CCC 1378). For a more detailed discussion of many of the issues covered in this chapter as well as other matters, see Thomas J. Nash, *The Biblical Roots of the Mass* (Manchester, NH: Sophia Institute Press, 2015), and Brant Pitre, *Jesus and the Jewish Roots of the Eucharist: Unlocking the Secrets of the Last Supper* (New York: Doubleday, 2011).

[10] I prefer to use the phrase "Sacrifice *of* Calvary"—or "Offering *of* Calvary" —rather than "Sacrifice *on* Calvary", because the events of Jesus' one Sacrifice are not limited to his Passion and Death *on* the Cross. This is a very important point to make, especially at the outset of this chapter.

[11] These properties would include the intoxicating qualities of wine and the negative effects of gluten on the gluten-intolerant.

the dead and ascended to the heavenly sanctuary—not a mere earthly Temple—and culminated his one Sacrifice in *everlasting glory* as the *heavenly high priest* (Heb. 8:1–3; 9:11–14). As the author of the Letter to the Hebrews summarizes so beautifully:

> Now the point in what we are saying is this: we have such a high priest, one who is seated at the right hand of the throne of the Majesty in heaven, a minister in the sanctuary and the true tent which is set up not by man but by the Lord. For every high priest is appointed to offer gifts and sacrifices; *hence it is necessary for this priest also to have something to offer.* . . . Christ has obtained a ministry which is as much more excellent than the old as the covenant he mediates is better, since it is enacted on better promises. For if that first covenant had been faultless, there would have been no occasion for a second (Heb. 8:1–3, 6–7, emphasis added).

> [W]hen Christ appeared as a high priest of the good things that have come, then through the greater and more perfect tent (not made with hands, that is, not of this creation) he entered once for all into the Holy Place, taking not the blood of goats and calves but his own blood, thus securing an eternal redemption. . . . Indeed, under the [Old Covenant] law, almost everything is purified with blood, and without the shedding of blood there is no forgiveness of sins.
>
> Thus it was necessary for the copies of the heavenly things to be purified with these rites, but the heavenly things themselves with better sacrifices than these. For Christ has entered, not into a sanctuary made with hands [i.e., the Temple], a copy of the true one, but into *heaven itself, now* to appear in the presence of God on our behalf (Heb. 9:11–12, 22–24, emphasis added).

Jesus, now and forever in heaven, *offers* himself to the Father in his risen humanity. The Son never stops giving himself to the Father, only now he does so in his immortal humanity on our behalf. So, to be clear, what is new at every Mass is not Jesus' Sacrifice, *but our participation anew in that one Sacrifice*, precisely because it is ever before the Father in the heavenly sanctuary; and so heaven and earth become extraordinarily one at each Mass.

Protestant Christians often speak of the "finished work of Christ,"[12] citing Jesus' words on the Cross right before he expired (see Jn. 19:30). They believe that we can draw on the fruits of Christ's Sacrifice of Calvary through the Sacrament of Baptism or "believer's baptism," for example, but that his all-important actual Sacrifice remains a historical thing of the past.

However, notice that the author of Hebrews says the prime function of a priest is to offer gifts and sacrifices (8:3), that Jesus holds his priesthood permanently (7:25), which means he needs to have something "to offer" (present tense) as a *heavenly* high priest (8:3). And that's why Jesus makes priestly intercession for us *now* (9:23–24), as well as because the heavenly sanctuary transcends the earthly limits of time. Well, if Jesus died once for all, which Scripture affirms he did (Heb. 7:27, 9:28), then either (1) Jesus is offering a *new* sacrifice in heaven, which would signal the inadequacy of his Sacrifice of Calvary; or (2) his one

---

[12] The Church would agree that Christ's atoning Passion and Death are finished, but that his one Sacrifice is not limited to the events of his Passion and Death.

Sacrifice, which began on earth, somehow *continues* in heaven, meaning that Jesus' Ascension to heaven was not simply a triumphant "drive home" after the sacrificial "finished work" of his Passion and Death.

The first option cannot be reconciled with Scripture, and no authentic Christian would espouse it. The second option, which the Church teaches (see CCC 662), is harmonious with Scripture. Suffice it to say for now that *there's no middle ground between the two options*, because Scripture makes clear that Jesus is a heavenly high priest and his one Sacrifice fulfills all Old Testament offerings,[13] including two which are crucial to understanding the Church's teaching on the Sacrifice of the Mass:

1. The Passover, which was a communion sacrifice,[14] in which lambs were slain in sacrifice and eaten at table annually by the Israelites (see Ex. 12); and

2. The annual Day-of-Atonement (*Yom Kippur*) sacrifices, in which the blood of a bull and a goat were offered for the sins of the high priest of Israel and the Israelites, respectively (see Lev. 16).[15]

---

[13] Heb. 10:14; see 10:1–18; Eph. 2:14; CCC 522; 2305.

[14] A communion sacrifice is one in which the sacrificial victim is both offered and eaten.

[15] Old Covenant sacrifices, which began with the formal establishment of Israel as a nation of God's people in Exodus 24, are a subset of the larger category of Old Testament sacrifices, which include Abel's offering of his first fruits (Gen. 4), Melchizedek's sacrifice of bread and wine (Gen. 14) and Abraham's offering of his son Isaac (Gen. 22).

Merely a Symbol or Something More?

Having provided an outline of the Church's teaching on the Eucharist/Mass, and with the promise that we will examine more closely Christ's fulfillment of the Passover and Day-of-Atonement sacrifices, we turn first to how the three main Reformers viewed the Eucharist/Lord's Supper. As noted briefly in the Introduction, Martin Luther and Ulrich Zwingli—who both once served as Catholic priests—differed sharply over the nature of the Eucharist. Zwingli believed the bread and wine are mere symbols of Christ's Body and Blood that do not change in any way at the Christian celebration of the Lord's Supper. When Jesus says, "This is my body" at the Last Supper, Zwingli concluded that "is" means "signified," not that Christ literally meant he was changing the bread and wine into his Body and Blood. In addition, because of limitations in Christ's human nature, Zwingli believed that Jesus' body could only be in one place, and so neither he nor anyone else could partake of it in a physical manner. Besides, based on Zwingli's reading of Jesus' words in John 6:63, a bodily reception of Jesus would not be spiritually profitable.

Consequently, Zwingli viewed the celebration of the Eucharist as a mere recollection of Christ's one Sacrifice, not a re-presentation or participation anew in that Sacrifice. And yet he also believed that Christians partake of Christ's Body in a spiritual manner in receiving the Eucharist, but he attributed that presence of Christ to the action of the Holy Spirit, not because of any change to the bread and wine. In that sense, one could say that Zwingli believed the celebration of the Lord's Supper provides an occasion of spiritual communion with Christ, but he did not see that partaking as strengthening faith or remitting sin, in contrast to Luther, but he did see it as providing spiritual comfort to believers (see Jn. 6:63).[16] *Zwingli's view of the Eucharist is the most common one among Protestant Christians today.*

John Calvin had a similar but higher view of the Eucharist than Zwingli. He denied that any substantive change takes place in the bread and wine and yet, unlike Zwingli, he believed that Christ's Body and Blood are spiritually present with the bread and wine that is consumed, and by the power of the Holy Spirit are brought from heaven to benefit only the predestined believers,[17] as they consume the sacrament and receive Christ's life: "For although Christ being elevated to heaven has left his abode on earth in which we are still pilgrims, yet no distance can dissolve his power of nourishing his own with himself."[18] "To summarize," Calvin wrote elsewhere, "the flesh and blood of Christ feed our souls just as bread and wine maintain and support our corporeal life."[19]

---

[16] Ulrich Zwingli, *On Providence and Other Essays*, Samuel Macauley Jackson and William John Hinke, eds. (Durham, NC: The Labyrinth Press, 1983), 252–53.

[17] For Calvin's view on predestination and the predestined believers, see Chapter 3.

[18] John Calvin, *Instruction in Faith (The Catechism)*. As cited in *Readings in Church History: Three Vols. in One*, rev. ed. (Westminster, MD: Christian Classics, Inc., 1985), 647.

[19] John Calvin, *The Institutes of the Christian Religion*, Henry Beveridge, trans., bk. 4, ch. 17, sect. 10; https://www.ccel.org/ccel/calvin/institutes.vi.xviii.html.

Luther had the highest view of the Eucharist among the three early Reformers. In contrast to the Catholic Church, Luther espoused "consubstantiation," i.e., that the bread and wine do not substantively change, but that Christ's Body and Blood are present "in and under" the elements of bread and wine.[20] Luther also taught that Christ's Body and Blood are only present for the duration of the liturgical service. Consequently, Lutherans don't reserve their post-service communion wafers, whereas Catholics do reserve the Blessed Sacrament in tabernacles, i.e., ornate containers that are often located behind the main altar in a church.[21]

Similar to the Catholic Church, Luther also taught that the Eucharist strengthens faith and remits sins,[22] but, like Zwingli and Calvin, Luther did not believe the Eucharist is a Sacrifice. To the Reformers, this Catholic teaching blasphemes Christ, as though it implies that Jesus' one Sacrifice

To access *The Institutes* more generally, see https://www.ccel.org/ccel/calvin/insti tutes.toc.html.

[20] Martin Luther, "The Sacrament of the Altar," *The Large Catechism*, no. 8; http://bookofconcord.org/lc-7-sacrament.php.

[21] Because Jesus is really present in the Blessed Sacrament, the Church makes available to the faithful "Eucharistic adoration," both when the sacrament is enclosed in the tabernacle and also exposed more formally in a monstrance, i.e., an ornate, typically gold stand in which the faithful can gaze upon and adore their Eucharistic Lord. In doing so, the Church emulates in a fulfilled manner the adoration the Old Covenant Israelites gave to God in the ancient Temple, who most intimately dwelled on earth within the holy of holies—the innermost portion of the Temple.

[22] Luther, "The Sacrament of the Altar," *The Large Catechism*, nos. 20–24; http://bookofconcord.org/lc-7-sacrament.php.

is not fully effective for the world's salvation. They unfortunately did not see the intimate connection between Christ's one Sacrifice for sin and its sacramental re-presentation in the Mass, a topic we will return to later in this chapter.

Still, the Eucharistic views of the Church and these early Reformers—Calvin and Luther in particular—are in some ways similar. Even though the Church does not recognize the validity of the Eucharists of Calvinists and Lutherans,[23] these two Reformers agreed with the Church that this sacrament has salvific power. For Luther and Calvin, and to a lesser extent Zwingli, they believed that the power of the Eucharist stemmed from the one Sacrifice of Calvary. Though the Reformers believed that Christ's work is totally finished, they would argue that the fruits of his Sacrifice are infinite and therefore available to benefit human persons until Jesus' Second Coming.

The Church agrees that the source and power of the Eucharist is Christ's one Sacrifice, but in a much more marvelous way. For the Church, the Eucharist allows the faithful to participate anew in the one Sacrifice of Christ in a sacramental way—where heaven and earth become mind-bogglingly one—instead of simply accessing a long-past sacrifice that still issues forth fruits.

In addition, the Church can agree with Zwingli and Calvin that Jesus is spiritually present in the Eucharist, but, again, in a much more sublime way than either of them taught, and in a way that exceeds Luther's view as well.

---

[23] In short, because Calvinists and Lutherans—following from their founders' teachings—don't view the Eucharist as a Sacrifice, it necessarily follows that they don't have validly ordained priests to consecrate the bread and wine.

Consistent with Jesus' words that his Body is real food and his Blood real drink (Jn. 6:55), the Church teaches that Jesus is corporeally or bodily present in the Eucharist, and yet *after the manner of a spirit.* What this means is that Jesus' Body, because it is united to his omnipotent divine person, is present in a whole and undivided manner in each and every Eucharistic Host, and thus in each and every part of each Host (see CCC 1377). For more on this transcendent mystery, which is crucial in answering the counterclaims of the Reformers and many Protestant Christians today, *see the Appendix.*

Offered *and* Eaten:
Jesus as the New Covenant Passover Lamb

Jesus is the New Covenant (NC) Passover Lamb, and so we might understandably anticipate that he would be— like his Passover predecessors in the Old Covenant (OC) —both sacrificed and consumed. Consider the parallels:

OC — Passover lamb had to be without blemish (Ex. 12:5).

NC — Christ is unblemished in a more important sense, i.e., like us in all things but sin (Heb. 4:15; 9:14).

OC — Break none of the lamb's bones (Ex. 12:46).

NC — So also with Jesus' bones (Jn. 19:36).

OC — Lamb is sacrificed/slaughtered and eaten (Ex. 12: 6–8).

NC — So also with Jesus, who is sacrificed/crucified (Mt. 16:21; Jn. 19:18) and eaten (Mt. 26:26–29).

OC — Offered lambs delivered Israel from the bondage of slavery (Ex. 12:1–13).

NC — Jesus delivers us from the much greater bondage of sin and spiritual death (Heb. 9:11–12).

John the Baptist identifies Jesus as the Lamb of God who takes away the sins of the world (Jn. 1:29, 36). (We hear those words repeated regularly at Mass during the _Agnus-Dei_ ["Lamb of God"] portion of the Eucharistic Prayer.) And St. Paul says that Christ our Pasch/Paschal Lamb has been sacrificed (1 Cor. 5:7). So why wouldn't we expect Jesus to be _both_ offered _and_ eaten like the Old Covenant Passover lambs? If Jesus were speaking in a merely figurative way at the Last Supper, the NC Passover would be a rather anticlimactic fulfillment of its OC predecessor. And thus the consumption of the Eucharist at Mass would be purely symbolic, or a slightly higher version of that, as consistent with Zwingli's perspective.

The Eucharist:
The Ultimate "Real Thing"

To further substantiate that we eat Jesus' Body and drink his Blood under the appearances of bread and wine at Catholic Masses, we will now turn to the extended scriptural passage that both Catholic and Protestant leaders address first in debating the nature of the Eucharist: the "Bread of Life Discourse" in John 6. If you're old enough to remember or perhaps have seen them on the Internet, you may recall the famous Coke commercials of the 1970s, in which a multicultural group of young people proclaim about the soft drink, "It's the real thing!"[24] Well, if we may elevate the theme a bit, the Eucharist could be described as "the ultimate Real Thing," in which Christ offers himself on behalf of the biggest multicultural group possible: the whole world (see Mt. 28:18–20; 1 Jn. 2:1–2).

The day after Jesus miraculously multiplies five loaves and two fish to feed a crowd that includes five thousand men (Jn. 6:10), he tells his disciples he will do something much more miraculous: multiply himself so that they can eat his Body and drink his Blood unto eternal life! *The multiplication of loaves is an indication to Zwingli, Calvin and like-minded Christians that if Jesus can greatly exceed the natural limits of several pieces of bread, why couldn't he do something remarkable with his own seemingly limited human body, given that it's united to his omnipotent divine person, instead of simply corporeally confining it to heaven?* (Again, see the Appendix for more on this important topic.)

Jesus chides those who follow him across the Sea of Galilee to Capernaum, saying, "Truly, truly, I say to you, you seek me, not because you saw signs, but because you ate your fill of the loaves. Do not labor for the food which perishes, but for the food which endures to eternal life, which the Son of man will give to you; for on him has God the Father set his seal" (Jn. 6:26–27). His Jewish disciples ask for a sign from Jesus to prove his worth, noting that Moses gave their ancestors manna, the "bread from heaven" that sustained them in their wilderness wanderings following the Exodus (Jn. 6:30–31). Jesus responds that he is the true bread from heaven and that he who comes to

---

[24] See, for example, https://www.youtube.com/watch?v=2msbfN81Gm0.

him will not hunger, and he who believes in him will never thirst (Jn. 6:32, 35). These words begin to alienate many of his followers. The remainder of the Bread of Life Discourse is worth quoting at length:

> The Jews then murmured at him, because he said, "I am the bread which came down from heaven." They said, "Is not this Jesus, the son of Joseph, whose father and mother we know? How does he now say, 'I have come down from heaven'?" Jesus answered them, "Do not murmur among yourselves. . . . Truly, truly I say to you, he who believes has eternal life. I am the bread of life. Your fathers ate the manna in the wilderness, and they died. This is the bread which comes down from heaven, that a man may eat of it and not die. I am the living bread which came down from heaven; if any one eats of this bread, he will live for ever; and the bread which I shall give for the life of the world is my flesh."
>
> The Jews then disputed among themselves, saying, "How can this man give us his flesh to eat?" So Jesus said to them, "Truly, truly, I say to you, unless you eat the flesh of the Son of man and drink his blood, you have no life in you; he who eats my flesh and drinks my blood has eternal life, and I will raise him up at the last day. For my flesh is food indeed, and my blood is drink indeed. He who eats my flesh and drinks my blood abides in me, and I in him. As the living Father sent me, and I live because of the Father, so he who eats me will live because of me. This is the bread which came down from heaven, not such as the fathers ate and died; he who eats this bread will live for ever." This he said in the synagogue, as he taught at Capernaum.
>
> Many of his disciples, when they heard it, said, "This is a hard saying; who can listen to it?" But Jesus, knowing in himself that his disciples murmured at it, said to them, "Do you take offense at this? Then what if you were to see the Son of man ascending where he was before? It is the Spirit that gives life, the flesh is of no avail; the words that I have

spoken to you are Spirit and life. But there are some of you that do not believe." For Jesus knew from the first who those were that did not believe, and who it was that would betray him. And he said, "This is why I told you that no one can come to me unless it is granted him by the Father."

After this many of his disciples drew back and no longer walked with him. Jesus said to the Twelve, "Will you also go away?" Simon Peter answered him, "Lord, to whom shall we go? You have the words of eternal life; and we have believed, and have come to know, that you are the Holy One of God" (Jn. 6:41–43; 47–69).

Notice that Jesus' hearers understand his words literally, *not* figuratively, when they ask him unbelievingly how he could give them his Flesh to eat (Jn. 6:52). Jesus does nothing to clarify that they're mistaken. Instead, Jesus makes his teaching on the Eucharist emphatic both by his *repetition* and *rhetorical* selection of words. To convey Christ's meaning regarding the word "eat," John first uses forms of the Greek word *esthio* through 6:53, a verb that describes the consumption of food. But then—for repetitive emphasis—he switches in 6:54, 56, 57 and 58 to *trogo*, a more graphic verb which literally means to "gnaw" or "chew."[25]

In response, his Jewish disciples *continue* to understand Jesus literally about eating his Flesh. But they have come to a crisis point, putting their alliance with Christ in doubt. As if to seek reassurance from Jesus that he is speaking figuratively, many of his disciples say aloud, "This is a hard

---

[25] See Paul R. McReynolds, *Word Study Greek-English New Testament* (Wheaton, IL: Tyndale House Publishers, Inc., 1998), 353–54. See also Spiros Zodhiates, ed., *The Hebrew-Greek Key Study Bible*—New American Standard Bible version (Chattanooga, TN: AMG Publishers), 1408; and p. 33, no. 2068, and p. 73, no. 5176, of the "Greek Dictionary of the New Testament" appendix.

saying; who can listen to it?" (Jn. 6:60). When there are misunderstandings elsewhere, Jesus provides clarity for his disciples. Consider Matthew 16:5–12. When his disciples think that "the leaven of the Pharisees and Sadducees" (Mt. 16:6) is actual bread, Jesus helps them to understand that he means their bad teaching.

But here in John 6 Jesus provides no clarification for his disciples, who don't want to believe that they would actually have to eat his Flesh and drink his Blood. And so many of his disciples choose no longer to walk with Jesus (Jn. 6:66).

Zwingli and others would counter that Jesus _does_ set the record straight when he says, "It is the Spirit that gives life, the flesh is of no avail" (Jn. 6:63). But those words don't comfort Jesus' followers, because many of them leave _after_ he says those words. The context of John 6 is very clear. When Jesus' disciples illustrate they understand him to be speaking literally and cannot accept his teaching, Jesus' response is to increasingly emphasize that he _is_ speaking literally. Indeed, when many of his disciples depart, Jesus does not call out and tell them that there's been a big misunderstanding. To the contrary, he simply and soberly asks his apostles, "Will you also go away?" (Jn. 6:67).

Regarding John 6:63, some Catholic biblical scholars argue that Jesus is telling his disciples that a spiritual view will enable them by faith to believe in his Eucharistic Real Presence, whereas an unspiritual and carnal perspective— i.e., "human judgment without faith"—will be of no avail.[26]

---

[26] Dom Ralph Russell, "St. John," in Rev. Reginald C. Fuller, et al., eds., A _New Commentary on Holy Scripture_, rev. and updat. ed. (New York: Thomas Nelson Publishers, 1975), p. 1051, no. 808m. See also Rev. W. Leonard, "The

In addition, I would argue that Zwingli and others miss how Jesus qualifies his words in 6:63 within the immediate context that reaffirms a literal understanding of his words:

> Many of his disciples, when they heard it, said, "This is a hard saying; who can listen to it?" *But Jesus, knowing in himself that his disciples murmured at it, said to them, "Do you take offense at this? Then what if you were to see the Son of man ascending where he was before?* It is the Spirit that gives life, the flesh is of no avail; the words that I have spoken to you are Spirit and life. *But there are some of you that do not believe*" (Jn. 6:60–64, emphases added).

In forecasting his Ascension "to where he was before," namely, with the Father in heaven, Jesus reaffirms his divine identity (see, e.g., Jn. 5:18; 8:58), to which some of his disciples refuse assent (Jn. 6:64). So I would argue that Jesus is conveying that his flesh, i.e., his human nature *by itself*, has no power to give life, eternal or otherwise. However, when united to his divine Person by the Holy Spirit at his Incarnation, and, more to the point, when it becomes present sacramentally as the Sacrifice of Calvary culminated in everlasting glory at Mass by the power of that same Spirit, it becomes a participant in a wondrous divine blessing (see Appendix). St. Cyril of Alexandria makes a similar argument, equating "the spirit that quickeneth" with Christ's divinity and "the flesh that profiteth nothing" with Christ's mere human nature on its own.[27]

Gospel of Jesus Christ According to St. John," in Dom Bernard Orchard, et al., eds., *A Catholic Commentary on Holy Scripture* (New York: Thomas Nelson & Sons, 1953), p. 994, no. 795h.

[27] As cited in Leonard, "The Gospel of Jesus Christ According to St. John," in *A Catholic Commentary on Holy Scripture*, p. 994, no. 795h. See also Pitre, *Jesus and the Jewish Roots of the Eucharist*, 107–11.

Further, why would Jesus' disciples "take offense" (Jn. 6:61) at his words if Jesus merely meant them in a non-offensive, figurative way? In addition, in response to the allegedly clarifying words of Jesus in John 6:63–64, his heretofore disbelieving disciples do not suddenly say, "Oh! Now we get it! You *are* speaking figuratively after all!" To the contrary, Jesus' "hard saying" (Jn. 6:60) remains hard as his disciples' departure attests (Jn. 6:66), affirming once more that the Lord is speaking literally.

Understanding an Idiom in Its Ancient Historical Context

Still, some critics will counter that when Jesus says that those who eat his Flesh and drink his Blood will have eternal life, he *must* be speaking figuratively, because earlier in his discourse he says, "Truly, truly I say to you, he who believes has eternal life" (Jn. 6:47). Thus, eating Jesus' Flesh is a figure of speech or idiom that simply means to believe in Jesus' teaching. Such an interpretation overlooks the aforementioned and overwhelming contextual evidence of John 6. In addition, one must interpret ancient idioms in their cultural context, making sure not to impose on the Gospel a modern meaning that is disconnected from a first-century, Jewish worldview.

To "eat the body and drink the blood," or "to devour my flesh," is a biblical expression that, when used in a nonliteral way, refers to hostile actions taken by an enemy who is intent on destroying another person (or at least their reputation). This is illustrated clearly in Psalm 27:2–3: "When evildoers come at me to devour my flesh, these my foes and my enemies themselves stumble and fall. Though an army encamp against me, my heart does not fear; though war be waged against me even then I will trust" (New American Bible; see Deut. 32:42). The Revised Standard Version Catholic Edition renders the passage, "When evildoers assail me, uttering slanders against me, my adversaries and foes, they shall stumble and fall" (Ps. 27:2), but explains in a footnote that what is translated as "uttering slanders against me" literally means "to eat up my flesh."

To "eat up someone's flesh," then, was a figurative way of saying you wanted to destroy or kill that person, or at least destroy their reputation through slander. Protestant scholars recognize the use of this ancient Hebrew idiom in Psalm 27:2, even if they don't take Jesus literally regarding the consumption of his Flesh in John 6.[28]

Consequently, if we insert a figurative meaning into John 6:54 that accurately represents the ancient Hebrew idiom, the passage is reduced to nonsense. Jesus is made to look like a pious yet demented masochist, or someone possessed by a demon: "He who kills me or slanders me has eternal life." The Jewish crowd gathered in Capernaum that day would have been aware of this familiar idiom, and thus would have understood how foolish Jesus would sound had he intended his words figuratively. They knew Jesus was an intelligent Jew and would not make such an obvious blunder. So his followers have difficulty with Jesus *not* because they think he's misusing an established cultural idiom, but because they understand him to be speaking literally. Indeed, the text of John 6 conveys that the crowd responds

---

[28] See, e.g., http://biblehub.com/commentaries/psalms/27-2.htm.

to Jesus as though he's speaking literally, and, for his part, Jesus says and does everything to reinforce a literal understanding among all those gathered.

St. Paul affirms a literal understanding of Jesus' teaching, saying that those who have eaten Christ's Body and Blood in an unworthy manner have gotten sick or died (1 Cor. 11:27–32). People don't get sick or die by consuming a small portion of mere bread or mere wine.

A Covenantal "Catch 22": Will Jesus' Jewish Disciples Drink His Blood?

As chapter six closes and chapter seven opens in John's Gospel, we read that Jesus begins to avoid Judea because the Jews sought to kill him (Jn. 7:1). Why? Because the Jews not only had prohibitions against eating human flesh, they also had laws against the consumption of blood (Gen. 9:4), the penalty for which a person—an Israelite or any foreigner who sojourned with Israel—would be cut off from God's people (Lev. 17:10–14). That's because God designated the blood of sacrificial animals to atone imperfectly for the sins of his people, noting that blood provides atonement because of the life that is in it. In short, to teach contrary to God's law was the sign of a false prophet (see Deut. 13:1–5), so the Jewish leaders sought Jesus' death because they saw his invitation to consume his Flesh and Blood as a grave violation of the Old Covenant.

However, the Mosaic legislation of the Old Covenant was *not* intended by God to last forever. Indeed, the prophet Jeremiah had foretold of a "New Covenant," implying that the old one God had made with Israel after liberating them from Egypt would be fulfilled (Jer. 31:31–34; see Ezek. 36:24–28). In bidding his apostles to eat his Body and drink his Blood, Jesus signals that the time had arrived to establish "the New Covenant in my blood" (Lk. 22:20).

Given the misperception that consuming the Eucharist would cut one off from Israel instead of fulfill the Old Covenant, Jesus' invitation to his first disciples required great faith. The blood of animal sacrifices reminded the Israelites of their need for atonement before God. Blood represented the life of the animal, which was given for the sake of man's life. Consumption of that animal blood, though, would draw them *downward*, fostering debased communion with those animals. In contrast, Jesus' Blood is a sacrament of divine life that would draw them *upward*, providing greater communion with Jesus and thus enabling them to become more like the Son of God. *This* is why Jesus commands his disciples, then and now, to drink his Blood.

The early Church's opponents testified that Christians took Jesus literally regarding the Eucharist. Roman pagans called early Church Christians "cannibals" precisely because the disciples spoke of *eating* and *drinking* their God. In doing so, the pagans provide further evidence that belief in the Real Presence of the Eucharist is an ancient Christian doctrine, and that the first Christians understood Jesus to be speaking *literally* when he established at the Last Supper the ritual we have come to call the Mass. Noting the attacks of the Roman historian Tacitus (circa A.D. 55 to circa A.D. 117) and others, Fr. Peter Stravinskas concludes:

Both Tertullian and Minucius Felix[29] . . . give considerable attention in their second-century writings to the charge of cannibalism being leveled against the Church. A belief in the Real Presence thus clearly existed in the early Church, for no "simple memorial supper" would have evoked such specific and violent charges from the general pagan populace.[30]

At the same time, the charge of cannibalism is misapplied to the Eucharist. Cannibals consume the flesh of a _dead_ person in a way that diminishes and profanes the person's corpse. With the Sacrament of the Eucharist, Jesus freely gives himself to us; and we consume his _living_, glorified Body and Blood in a way that mysteriously and miraculously does not diminish him. (For a more in-depth treatment of this aspect of the Eucharistic Mystery, see the Appendix).

The "Gift that Keeps on Giving": The Once-for-All Sacrifice of Jesus

To understand how Jesus' Sacrifice did not begin and end on that first Good Friday, we need to examine more closely the annual Old Covenant Day of Atonement sacrifices, which had two primary phases: (1) the slaughter of the victims and (2) the sprinkling of their blood in the Temple's holy of holies, both of which are described in Leviticus 16. In the first phase, a bull was slaughtered for the high priest's sins and a goat for the people's sins on the Temple's altar of sacrifice. In the second phase, the high priest would take

---

[29] Tertullian and Minucius Felix were both early Christian writers.

[30] Fr. Peter Stravinskas, _The Catholic Response_ (Huntington, IN: Our Sunday Visitor, 1985), 91.

the blood of the bull and the goat beyond the sanctuary veil into the holy of holies—the innermost chamber of the Temple—and sprinkle that blood on and before the mercy seat of God atop the Ark of the Covenant.[31] In the theology of Israel, the Ark was the earthly throne of God, the seat of his most intimate presence in the world.

Only the high priest could enter the holy of holies, and he could only do so *once* a year. To do so on any other day of the year would result in death, whether his or anyone else's (Lev. 16:1–2; Num. 3:10; 18:7).[32] This ordinance served as a reminder of the rupture between God and man that had begun in the Garden of Eden, a rupture which Christ had come to remedy.

Jesus fulfills the Day of Atonement sacrifices. His Sacrifice also has two phases. In the first or earthly phase, Jesus suffers, dies and rises from the dead as priest and victim. In

---

[31] The Ark of the Covenant contained the tablets of the Ten Commandments, Aaron's priestly staff that budded and some manna from the desert in a golden urn (Heb. 9:4). It is perhaps best known in modern times as the focus of the cinematic blockbuster "Raiders of the Lost Ark."

[32] That the Israelites would die in wrongfully entering the holy of holies should give anyone pause in receiving Jesus in the Eucharist, also known as "Holy Communion," or even walking casually through the sanctuary, indifferent to Christ's Real Presence in the tabernacle. By defeating sin and death, Jesus tore in two—from top to bottom—the Temple curtain that enclosed the holy of holies (Mt. 27:51), signifying that God's people could now draw near to have intimate communion with the Father, Son and Holy Spirit. Adam and Eve didn't immediately die a physical death in sinning against God, but, contrary to what the devil promised, they died a much more important spiritual death, because they were alienated from God. Similarly, those who receive the Eucharist in mortal sin may not physically die, but they compound the gravity of their spiritually dead condition and should repent by receiving the Sacrament of Reconciliation as soon as possible.

the second or heavenly phase, Jesus ascends into heaven as the New Covenant high priest, taking not the inferior blood of goats and calves, which had to be offered year after year, but *his own blood*. And he takes his blood not into a mere earthly Temple, but into the *heavenly* holy of holies, thus securing an eternal redemption (Heb. 9:11–12).

In addition, in the Old Covenant, the slaughter of the victims took place in the outer court of the Temple sanctuary, visible to the people, whereas the offering of their blood for atonement took place in the innermost chamber of the sanctuary, concealed from all human eyes, except the high priest. Similarly, the Passion and Death of Jesus was a public spectacle, whereas his Ascension completes the liturgy of atonement, since this is when Jesus—fully possessed of his body and blood once again as the *perfect high priest*—takes his humanity beyond the veil of visible creation into the hidden throne room of God in heaven.

To review, Jesus holds his priesthood permanently (Heb. 7:23–25). He is a priest in heaven and therefore must offer a sacrifice, because that's what priests do (Heb. 8:1–3). And so he makes intercession for us *now* with the Father (Heb. 9:24). In addition, a "sacrifice of atonement" entails *shedding* blood *and then offering* that blood before the throne of God, represented by the Ark of the Covenant in the Old Covenant and the heavenly sanctuary in the New. So a complete sacrifice of atonement requires *both*, just as we explored earlier that a complete participation in the Passover requires both a blood sacrifice and a communion meal.

Further, a self-sacrifice can continue when the victim

rises from the dead. And, in Jesus' case, because it culminated in everlasting glory in the heavenly sanctuary, we see that his Sacrifice is *never-ending*, truly the ultimate "Gift that keeps on giving"—*forever*. In other words, the Sacrifice of Jesus cannot be repeated *because* it is *perpetual*, now caught up into eternity. In addition, because we partake of Jesus, the New Covenant Passover Lamb, the Mass is the perfect Communion Sacrifice as well.

But how does Jesus' Sacrifice become present on earth at Mass?

Sacrifices to "Remember"

In the United States, we have a limited concept of remembering. Take the Fourth of July (Independence Day), for example, in which we celebrate our freedoms in the present while remembering the birth of our nation in 1776. We might even dress up as colonists and pretend to sign the Declaration of Independence. But the *past* remains in the *past*. The signing ceremony at Independence Hall in Philadelphia in 1776 doesn't time-travel to the present, so that we can see John Hancock pen his famous signature. Our experience is a mere *recollection*. We don't have actual contact with the original event.

The concept of "memorial" or "remembrance" had much more significance for the ancient Israelites. The Passover Sacrifice was a "memorial." But not a mere recollection. "Memorial" meant something much more powerful—calling forth the power of a past event and feeling its impact in the present.

But how?

Old Covenant Passover lambs were "one and done." They could only be sacrificed once. And Old Covenant priests could only serve from ages 30 to 50. But _God's_ involvement was _trans-historical._ That is, God's original Passover blessing was timeless; it kept on giving. _Because God is not limited by time._ He created time, after all. It's kind of like the fallacy, "If God can do anything, can he make a rock so big that he can't pick it up?" A quick way to refute this fallacy is to ask, "Do you mean can someone who is unlimited be limited? Because if you grant as true that God can do anything as you have, then he can't be limited. And so what you propose in your question is something logically untenable, something that isn't or can't be real." Or, in other words, an omnipotent creator can't be limited by anything he creates. Similarly, God cannot be limited by time. So while each annual Passover required lots of new lambs, and the human priests would have to be replaced periodically as well, God could make his original Passover blessing present _anew_ 100 years later, 500 years later, 1,000 years later and so on.

In the New Covenant Passover, "remembrance" is even more stupendous. Because there's only:

- One Lamb: Jesus.
- One priest: Also Jesus.
- And Jesus happens to be . . . God (see Rev. 5:6, 12).

Consequently, in the New Covenant, _one_ Sacrifice suffices. And not only are we brought to the foot of the Cross _in mystery,_ because Jesus doesn't suffer anew, but also into the heavenly sanctuary, where Jesus intercedes for us _now._ Indeed, in heaven, Jesus is the "Lamb standing, as though it had been slain" (Rev. 5:6), bringing the totality of his one Sacrifice to the Father on our behalf. He bears the marks of his Passion and Death ("slain"), yet is "standing" because of his triumphant Resurrection and Ascension!

Phoenix vs. Sun Analogies

How can we understand even better that heaven and earth become one in the Eucharistic Liturgy? Some Christians think Catholics actually believe that we crucify Jesus at every Mass, or at least that we would have to do so if our teaching regarding the Mass and the Eucharist were true. This perspective reflects the phoenix analogy, aptly named for the ancient mythical bird that would arise from its ashes each day. But, as we discussed earlier, Scripture says that Jesus died "once for all" (Heb. 7:27; 9:28). And Jesus says of his atoning suffering, "It is finished" (Jn. 19:30).

So the phoenix analogy won't work. But consider the sun analogy. Relative to us, the sun rises in the east every day. Yet, even when it's dark outside, the sun is always "on." Otherwise, we'd all freeze to death here on earth. Even when we can't see it, the sun is and remains our earthly life source. And so, in contrast to the phoenix analogy, we don't have a brand-new sun at every sunrise. Instead, it's the same sun—day after day, year after year.

So what's new each day is not the sun, but *our experience* of the sun.

Similarly, in fulfilling the Day of Atonement sacrifices, Jesus rises from the dead and ascends into the heavenly holy of holies, where he lives to make priestly intercession for us *always* (Heb. 7:23–25). In other words Christ's one Sacrifice, similar to the sun in relation to us here on earth, is always "going on" in heaven, because we know that Jesus makes intercession for us *now* (Heb. 9:24).

In that light, the Mass is our "window onto eternity," our daily "sunrise"! And so we see again that what is new at every Mass is *not* Christ's Sacrifice, but—because time is joined to eternity by God's Providence—*our participation in offering anew* that *one* Sacrifice.

On Earth as It Is in Heaven:
The Priesthood According to the Order of Melchizedek

Finally, in what way does Christ's Sacrifice become present to us at Mass? According to the order of Melchizedek. "Who's Melchizedek?" you may be wondering. He makes a brief cameo in Genesis 14:17–20. He is an ancient high priest who offers bread and wine, and to whom the great patriarch Abraham gives tithes. Some say bread and wine aren't the "rite stuff" of sacrifices, pun intended. *That's not true.* Exodus 29:40 and other scriptural passages show that bread and wine can serve as offerings.

In Hebrews 5:1, similar to Hebrews 8:3, we read that "priests are appointed to offer gifts and sacrifices." We are reminded, then, that the prime function of a priest is to offer gifts and sacrifices. So if Melchizedek is making a brief cameo, and he's a high priest, and the prime function of a priest is to offer gifts and sacrifices, wouldn't it make sense that he'd be offering . . . a sacrifice? And that, because nothing else is mentioned, his offering would be bread and wine? And we know from the Last Supper accounts and John 6 that Jesus offers his Body and Blood *under the appearances of bread and wine*. So isn't it logical that Jesus is called . . . "a priest for ever, according to the order of Melchizedek"?![33]

A passage in the Letter to the Hebrews sublimely links Christ's living out his Sacrifice of Calvary with his Melchizedekian priesthood:

> In the days of his flesh, Jesus offered up prayers and supplications, with loud cries and tears, to him who was able to save him from death, and he was heard for his godly fear. Although he was a Son, he learned obedience through what he suffered; *and being made perfect he became the source of eternal salvation to all who obey him, being designated by God a high priest according to the order of Melchizedek* (Heb. 5:7–10, emphasis added).

The Letter to the Hebrews establishes a close connection between the Last Supper and Jesus' one Sacrifice of Calvary. That Christ's being designated a priest according to the order of Melchizedek is *intimately* and *inextricably* linked with his one priestly Sacrifice of Calvary. And thus that Jesus will *continue* his priestly ministry, his work of eternal salvation, *according to the order of Melchizedek*. Recall that at the Last Supper Jesus tells his apostles, "Do this in remembrance of me"[34] (Lk. 22:19–20; 1 Cor. 11:23–26) after consecrating *the bread and wine*.

---

[33] Heb. 5:6.

[34] Again, In English Masses of the Latin/Roman Rite, the word is translated as "memory."

So what happens at Mass? Heaven and earth *become one*. Jesus' one Sacrifice that culminated in everlasting glory . . . becomes present on altars worldwide through the power Christ imparts to his priests at their ordination (CCC 1566),[35] as they offer anew that one Sacrifice on their behalf and ours, and we also partake anew of the same sacrificial Passover Lamb of God who takes away the sins of the world, consuming his Body and Blood that we might have eternal life. And Jesus is made present according to the order of Melchizedek, i.e., under the appearances of bread and wine.

"Thy kingdom come, thy will be done, on earth as it is in heaven." Nowhere are these words of the Lord's Prayer

---

[35] The Church teaches that Jesus instituted the ministerial priesthood at the Last Supper, ordaining his Apostles so that they could carry on his Melchizedekian priesthood in sacramentally offering anew his one Sacrifice "in remembrance" of him (see CCC 874–77). In *Credo of the People of God*, a motu proprio published in 1968, Pope Paul VI succinctly summarizes the truly awesome role a priest plays at Mass:

> We believe that the Mass, celebrated by the priest representing the person of Christ by virtue of the power received through the Sacrament of Orders, and offered by him in the name of Christ and the members of His Mystical Body, is in true reality the Sacrifice of Calvary, rendered sacramentally present on our altars. We believe that as the bread and wine consecrated by the Lord at the Last Supper were changed into His body and His blood which were to be offered for us on the cross, likewise the bread and wine consecrated by the priest are changed into the body and blood of Christ enthroned gloriously in heaven, and we believe that the mysterious presence of the Lord, under what continues to appear to our senses as before, is a true, real and substantial presence (no. 24); http://w2.vatican.va/content/paul-vi/en/motu_proprio/documents/hf_p-vi_motu-proprio_19680630_credo.html.

more profoundly fulfilled than in the Mass! That is, when we have eyes to see and ears to hear, paradise/heaven *is as close as your local parish church*, and receiving Jesus in the Eucharist provides a foretaste of the heavenly "marriage supper of the Lamb"! (Rev. 19:9).

5

How Many Airborne Divisions Does the Church Militant Got?

A Celestial Army of Angels and Saints

To help us navigate the highway to heaven successfully, God gives us prayerful "air support" from those who have preceded us in death and are now in heaven.[1] Beginning at the Reformation, Protestant Christians have objected to the intercessory role that the Church teaches the angels and saints[2] play in our quest for eternal paradise, arguing that it encroaches upon Jesus Christ's role as the one mediator between God and man (see 1 Tim. 2:5). Before

---

[1] The saints in heaven from whom the faithful ask prayers would be clearly those who have been canonized by the Church. Sometimes Catholics privately ask for the intercession of faithful-departed friends and family, although, if they do, they should never presume they're in heaven and thereby neglect to offer Masses and other prayers for them. Some theologians, like St. Robert Bellarmine and St. Alphonsus Liguori, argue that Christians in Purgatory can intercede for us, though the Church has not pronounced on the matter; http://www.newadvent.org/cathen/12575a.htm. In any event, the faithful on earth should pray for the expeditious purification of the souls in Purgatory (see CCC 1030–32). For more on Purgatory, see Chapter 6.

In addition, there is a very important point to make: Like God himself, the angels and saints are available to help any Christian or non-Christian, not simply Catholics.

[2] The word "saints" can refer to any member of the Church, but I will employ the term in its most common Catholic use—describing the saints in heaven.

addressing this and other objections, let's first consider where Catholics have common ground with the Reformers on the greatest of saints: Mary, the Blessed Mother of Jesus.

Many Protestant Christians today would be shocked to discover that the early Reformers basically[3] affirmed the Church's four Marian dogmas, i.e., Mary's Perpetual Virginity, her Immaculate Conception,[4] her glorious Assumption (body and soul) into heaven, and her being the Mother of God. While many modern-day Protestants affirm that Mary conceived Jesus by the power of the Holy Spirit, it is also common to hear Protestants claim that Mary and Joseph naturally conceived children thereafter. But this was not always so. In responding to the fourth-century theologian Helvidius,[5] John Calvin affirmed that the "brothers and sisters of Jesus" in the Gospels refer to Our Lord's cousins, not children procreated by Mary and Joseph:

> The word _brothers_, we have formerly mentioned, is employed, agreeably to the Hebrew idiom, to denote any relatives whatever; and, accordingly, _Helvidius_ displayed excessive ignorance in concluding that Mary must have had many sons, because Christ's _brothers_ are sometimes mentioned.[6]

---

[3] "Basically" is used because Luther, for example, recognized Mary's Immaculate Conception according to the formula of his day and wasn't sure on the Assumption. See footnote 7 below. See also Catholics United for the Faith (CUF) Faith Fact on "Mary's Perpetual Virginity"; http://www.cuf.org/2004/04/marys-perpetual-virginity/.

[4] This Catholic dogma refers to _Mary's_ being conceived without sin, not her conception of Jesus, even though as the God-man he was conceived without sin as well. Mary was preserved from even the stain of original sin so that she could be a most fitting mother for Jesus.

[5] Helvidius' position was novel and quickly condemned by the great Scripture scholar St. Jerome.

[6] John Calvin, _Commentary on Matthew, Mark and Luke_, Vol. 2, "Matthew

Nor did the Reformers have issues with Mary's being called the "Mother of God." Adds Max Thurian, while still a Protestant:

> In regard to the Marian doctrine of the Reformers, we have already seen how unanimous they are in all that concerns Mary's holiness and perpetual virginity. Whatever the theological position which we may hold today in regard to the Immaculate Conception and Assumption of Mary . . . these two Catholic dogmas were accepted by certain Reformers, not of course in their present form, but certainly in the form current in their day.[7]

Understanding the Communion of Saints

In professing the Apostles' Creed, we say that we believe in "the holy catholic[8] Church" and "the communion of

---

13:53–58; Mark 6:1–6," emphases original; http://www.ccel.org/ccel/calvin/cal com32.ii.xxxix.html. See also Calvin's *Commentary on Matthew, Mark and Luke, Vol. 1,* "Matthew 1:18–25" in regard to Jesus as Mary's "firstborn" and also regarding Joseph as not having relations with Mary "until" Jesus was born; http://www.ccel.org/ccel/calvin/calcom31.ix.xv.html.

[7] Max Thurian, *Mary, Mother of All Christians* (New York: Herder and Herder, 1964), 197. As cited in Father Mateo, *Refuting the Attack on Mary: A Defense of Marian Doctrines* (San Diego, CA: Catholic Answers, 1993), 6.

As Catholic apologist Dave Armstrong reports, Martin Luther taught that Mary was purified from original sin at the moment she conceived Jesus (Armstrong, "Martin Luther's 'Immaculate Purification' View of Mary," *National Catholic Register,* December 31, 2016). Luther's position was very similar to that of St. Thomas Aquinas; http://www.ncregister.com/blog/darmstrong/martin-luthers-immaculate-purification-view-of-mary. In 1854, Pope Pius IX solemnly defined the dogma of Mary's Immaculate Conception, which refers to Mary's being conceived without sin, *not* the sinless conception of Jesus. And while Luther was uncertain regarding Mary's Assumption into heaven, he consistently called the Blessed Mother "the Queen of Heaven."

[8] The word "catholic" is lowercased in both the Apostles' and Nicene Creeds,

saints." These two terms touch upon the same reality, although sometimes people mistakenly think "the Church" refers only to Catholics who are here on earth. Actually, the Church is made up of the Church Militant (those advancing God's kingdom on earth), the Church Suffering (those being purified in Purgatory), and the Church Triumphant, i.e., the saints in heaven (CCC 946–59). And though the Church is confined to human persons redeemed by Christ, angels[9] are members of the larger family of God and thus on our side in helping us "fight the good fight" to attain heaven.

Because the Church Suffering and Church Triumphant, as well as the angels, are beyond this world, I good-naturedly refer to them as a celestial army. And obviously Jesus Christ is the divine general of the entire "army" of the family of God.[10]

---

because it refers to the Church's mark of "catholicity" or "universality," not the Church's formal title (see CCC 811–12; 830ff.)

[9] Here I obviously refer to the angels in heaven, not the fallen angels (demons) who rejected God and seek man's damnation (see CCC 327–30; 391–95).

[10] Also, the title of this chapter is a play on the infamous words that Soviet leader Joseph Stalin once pronounced about Pope Pius XI, which British Prime Minister Winston Churchill later recalled. In 1935, Stalin met with French Foreign Minister Pierre Laval, asking Laval what would be the strength of the French Army on the Western Front, including how many divisions and for what time period. After responding to Stalin's inquiry, Laval diplomatically alluded to Stalin's oppression and atrocities against Catholics, which included the genocidal starvation of millions just a couple of years earlier in Soviet Ukraine. "Can't you do something to encourage religion and the Catholics in Russia?" Laval asked. "It would help me so much with the Pope." "Oho! The Pope!" Stalin scoffed. "How many divisions has _he_ got?" the Soviet leader added, making his own allusion to the pontiff's lack of a conventional army. Said Churchill later, "Laval's answer was not reported to me; but he might certainly have mentioned a number of legions not always visible on parade" (Winston S. Churchill, The

Calvin harshly opposed prayer to the saints:

> I ask if this is not to transfer to them that office of sole inter-
> cession which we have above claimed for Christ? . . . [A]s if
> they supposed that Christ were insufficient or too rigorous.
> By this anxiety they dishonour Christ, and rob him of his title
> of sole Mediator. By so doing they obscure the glory of his
> nativity and make void his cross; in short, divest and defraud
> of due praise everything which he did or suffered, since all
> which he did and suffered goes to show that he is and ought
> to be deemed sole Mediator.[11]

Protestant Christians often also ask, why seek the help
of a saint when you can go directly to Jesus? Well, as is
often the case, the Catholic response is that it's a both/and,
not an either/or, because that's the way God set things up.
Obviously the saints aren't in a better position than Jesus
to intercede for us. The real issue is whether they can intercede for us, rooted in Christ; and if they can, wouldn't
it make sense to ask for their prayers as we do our fellow
Christians here on earth?

The Catholic Church teaches that any intercessory efforts by the saints and angels are only made *in and through*
Christ as the one mediator between God and man, and
therefore by the merits of his one Sacrifice of Calvary. In
addition, because they have finished their journey of faith
and thus are *in heaven*, the saints are in a more powerful
position to interact with God than any of us here on earth.
So *both* praying to God directly *and* asking the saints to

Gathering Storm: The Second World War, Vol. 1 [Boston: Houghton Mifflin Company, 1948], 121; emphasis original).

[11] John Calvin, *The Institutes of the Christian Religion*, bk. 3, ch. 20, sect. 21;
https://www.ccel.org/ccel/calvin/institutes.v.xxi.html.

bring our prayers to God will increase the impact of our efforts, and St. Paul further attests that God grants blessings "in answer to many prayers" (2 Cor. 1:11).

Moreover, as Catholic apologist Patrick Madrid notes, Calvin is being inconsistent in his criticism of the Church's teaching on intercessory prayer:

> If asking for the prayers of saints in heaven evidences an attitude that Christ's mediation is "insufficient or too rigorous," then asking *any Christian here on earth* for intercessory prayer is likewise an indictment of the sufficiency of Christ's mediation. . . . [So] if 1 Timothy 2:5 eliminates intercession by the Christians in heaven, it eliminates intercession by Christians on earth. . . . Yet, Calvin (like all Protestants) rightly allowed for and even extolled the practice of Christians on earth offering intercessory prayer for each other. Clearly, asking another Christian for intercessory prayer in no way indicates any lack of confidence in Christ.[12]

Nor would it make void Christ's redeeming work. Jesus himself urges intercessory prayer, including praying for our persecutors (Mt. 5:44). And those prayers, like other good works, are only efficacious in and through Christ. As Jesus teaches, he is the vine apart from whom we can bear no good fruit (Jn. 15:1–5). And that's why St. Paul—*right before describing Jesus as the one mediator in his First Letter to Timothy, no less*—exhorts his fellow Christians to intercede in prayer for everyone:

> I urge that supplications, prayers, intercessions, and thanksgivings be made for all men. . . .

---

[12] Patrick Madrid, *Any Friend of God Is a Friend of Mine: A Biblical and Historical Explanation of the Catholic Doctrine of the Communion of Saints* (San Diego, CA: Basilica Press, 1996), 18, 46, emphasis original.

> *This is good, and it is acceptable in the sight of God our Savior,* who desires all men to be saved and to come to the knowledge of the truth. For there is one God, and there is one mediator between God and men, the man Christ Jesus . . . (1 Tim. 2:1, 3–5, emphasis added).

The Saints:
Collaborators with God, Not Competitors

So we see that the *collaborative* mediation of the saints in heaven is rooted in and made possible by Christ, and brings Jesus further glory instead of detracting from his role as the one mediator between God and man. And while some argue it's impossible—from an earthly vantage point—for Mary and the other saints to receive simultaneously and deliver to Christ a multitude of prayers—those in heaven are not limited by the constraints of time and space, and they are otherwise empowered by Christ, to whom they are far closer than they were on earth. Indeed, Madrid argues, if St. Paul showed great loving concern for the salvation of others while he lived on earth (see Rom. 10:1), "is there any reason to imagine that upon entering heaven Paul's charity and desire for others' salvation would be quenched and his prayers for others cease? Not at all. The Bible's many exhortations to mutual charity apply to *all* Christians," adds Madrid, "so they must apply to Christians in heaven."[13] And if the prayer of a righteous man *on earth* avails much with God (Jas. 5:16–18), how much more would prayers from one who has finished the race and now reigns with Christ *in heaven?*

---

[13] Ibid., 38, emphasis original.

145

Another criticism of Church teaching is that asking for prayers from Christians who have died is tantamount to necromancy, or conjuring dead spirits, which the Bible condemns (e.g., Deut. 18:10–12; 1 Sam. 28:3–19). Necromancy is the occult practice of inquiring into the future or attempting to influence events by communicating with the spirits of the dead. It is categorically condemned by the Church (CCC 2115–17).

Praying to the saints is something wholly—and holy!— different. In response to the Sadducees, who did not believe in the resurrection of the dead, Jesus proclaims that those who die in God's fellowship *live on* in God, vs. only coming back to life when their bodies and souls are reunited at the end of time: "[H]ave you not read what was said to you by God, 'I am the God of Abraham, and the God of Isaac, and the God of Jacob'? He is not God of the dead, but of the living" (Mt. 22:31–32). That's why Jesus could converse with Moses and Elijah—who had died many years before —at the Transfiguration, a miraculous event that only Sts. Peter, James and John were privileged to see (Mt. 17:1–8).

Similarly, St. Paul teaches that all Christians are intimately united in Christ's Mystical Body, without making any exception for those who have died: "For as in one body we have many members, and all the members do not have the same function, so we, though many, are one body in Christ, and individually members one of another" (Rom. 12:4–5; see 1 Cor. 12:12). Given this intimate and unbreakable unity in Christ, Paul adds, "the members . . . have the same care for one another. If one member suffers, all suffer together; if one member is honored, all rejoice together"

(1 Cor. 12:25–26). Indeed, death cannot separate us from "the love of God *in Christ Jesus* our Lord" (Rom. 8:38–39, emphasis added). And since we are one body *in Christ Jesus*, death cannot separate us *from each other*.

Consequently, Jesus says, as a shepherd rejoices over finding a lost sheep, "Just so, I tell you, *there will be more joy in heaven* over one sinner who repents than over ninety-nine righteous persons who need no repentance." And as a woman rejoices in finding her lost silver coin, "Just so, I tell you, there is joy before the angels of God over one sinner who repents" (Lk. 15:7, 10).

Some might counter that Jesus mentions in Luke 15 the angels, but not specifically the saints. St. John provides clarifying insight in the Book of Revelation. In his vision of heaven, John writes, "the four living creatures and *the twenty-four elders* fell down before the Lamb, each holding a harp, *and with golden bowls full of incense, which are the prayers of the saints* . . ." (Rev. 5:8, emphases added). The 24 elders are *not* angels. They can only be human persons, Christians who have died and are now *in heaven*. And John presents them as clearly *mediating* the prayers of the saints *on earth*, because the elders present the bowls filled with prayers to Jesus the Lamb, the one mediator. Note well that these prayers don't go *directly* to Jesus; they are *brought* to him by the *mediating efforts* of the saintly elders (see Rev. 8:3).

And these intercessory prayers are undoubtedly powerful, because they are delivered to God by "the assembly of the firstborn who are enrolled in heaven" and "the spirits of just men *made perfect*" (Heb. 12:23, emphasis added). The "firstborn" are the Christians who have attained heaven, whereas "just men" may refer to the righteous men and women of Old Testament times who have been made perfect in Christ.[14] In any event, we know that "the firstborn" have been perfected in Christ, having gained heaven, and are thus in a more powerful position to intercede on our behalf than our brothers and sisters in Christ here on earth, though we should ask for their prayers as well.

The Letter to the Hebrews further affirms that the faithful departed in heaven are concerned with our spiritual well-being. After enumerating the various luminaries of salvation history in chapter 11, the author begins chapter 12 by speaking collectively of these biblical heroes who have gone before us:

> Therefore, _since we are surrounded by so great a cloud of witnesses_, let us also lay aside every weight, and sin which clings so closely, and let us run with perseverance the race that is set before us, looking to Jesus the pioneer and perfecter of our faith, who for the joy that was set before him endured the cross, despising the shame, and is seated at the right hand of the throne of God (Heb. 12:1–2, emphasis added).

"They are pictured crowded into a stadium, looking down on believers still running the race of faith and urging them on to victory," _The Ignatius Catholic Study Bible New Testament_ says of this great throng of heavenly witnesses:

> At the finish line stands Jesus, waiting to reward us (12:2). Images of the faithful departed cheering us on hint at the

---

[14] _The Ignatius Catholic Study Bible New Testament_ (San Francisco: Ignatius Press, 2010), 435.

communion and intercession of the saints. It shows that the Church in heaven is neither cut off from nor disinterested in the pilgrim Church on earth but is actively solicitous of her salvation (CCC 2683).[15]

Worshipping Statues, Dead Men's Bones and the Blessed Mother???

When Catholics kneel before the statue of a saint, they are not worshipping the person depicted, let alone the stone or plaster image as such. Catholics don't pray *to* images; they pray *through* them to the holy persons who are depicted. Sacred images help the faithful focus their minds and hearts when asking for a particular saint's intercession. In other words, these images are *instruments* of prayer, not *objects* of prayer in the strict sense.

By God's grace, the intercessory power of the saints can extend to their relics, including their worldly remains and items they owned while living on earth. This is not idolatry, but, again, a biblically rooted practice. Consider that a dead man came back to life when his corpse came in contact with the bones of Elisha (2 Kgs. 13:20–21); simply touching Jesus' garment cured a woman of a longstanding affliction with hemorrhages (Lk. 8:42–48); and handkerchiefs and aprons that St. Paul distributed resulted in the sick being healed and the possessed being exorcised (Acts 19:11–12). Again, *none of this is possible without Christ*, who advances

---

[15] Ibid., 433.

his kingdom through the collaboration of his saintly disciples.

As noted earlier, Mary the Mother of God is the greatest of the saints. While Martin Luther didn't believe in praying to the saints in heaven, he spoke of the Blessed Mother in glowing terms long after he renounced the Catholic Church, because she personifies par excellence what is possible for a disciple of Christ:

> She, the lady above heaven and earth, must . . . have a heart so humble that she might have no shame in washing the swaddling clothes or preparing a bath for St. John the Baptist, like a servant girl. What humility! It would surely have been more just to have arranged for her a golden coach, pulled by 4,000 horses, and to cry and proclaim as the carriage proceeded,
>
> "Here passes the woman who is raised above the whole human race!" . . . She was not filled with pride by this praise . . . this immense praise: "No woman is like unto thee! Thou art more than an empress or a queen . . . blessed above all nobility, wisdom, or saintliness!"[16]

In Old Covenant Israel, it was _the mother_ of the king who reigned with her son, _not_ the king's wife. The queen mother or _gebirah_—"great lady"—consequently had special power, including intercessory influence with the king.[17] Maacah, the mother of King Asa, was removed from her role as

---

[16] _Luther's Works_ Vol. 21, 327; Vol. 36, 208; Vol. 45, 107.

[17] Scott Hahn, _Hail, Holy Queen: The Mother of God in the Word of God_ (New York: Doubleday, 2001), 79; see 78–85. See also Tim Staples, _Behold Your Mother: A Biblical and Historical Defense of the Marian Doctrines_ (El Cajon, CA: Catholic Answers, 2014), 273–80; and Edward Sri, _Queen Mother: A Biblical Theology of Mary's Queenship_ (Steubenville, OH: Emmaus Road Publishing, 2005).

queen mother for making an image of the pagan goddess Asherah (2 Chron. 15:16). And Adonijah tried to use the influence of the Queen Mother Bathsheba to get his half-brother Solomon[18] to give him as his wife Abishag the Shunammite, who served their father King David in his old age (1 Kings 2:13–23; see 1 Kings 1:11–16, 22). "He will not refuse you," Adonijah says to Bathsheba, alluding to her intercessory prerogative. Adonijah's statement implies that —under normal circumstances—the queen mother's request carried great weight with the king, although all decisions ultimately rested with Israel's royal leader. Solomon saw through his half-brother's ploy to use his (Solomon's) mother and her position of power to topple him, and so he consequently killed Adonijah.

In the New Covenant kingdom of heaven, Mary is perfectly in sync with her Son, the King of kings. In addition, Mary is not simply the Queen Mother of Jesus; she is also our spiritual mother. "Behold, your mother!" Jesus proclaims from the Cross, in giving Mary to the beloved disciple, St. John, who symbolizes all Christians (Jn. 19:27). Thus, we are "her offspring," we who strive to "keep the commandments of God and bear testimony to Jesus" (Rev. 12:17).

The family of God extends well beyond this world. Mary and the saints and angels are God's friends, given to help us receive and persevere in his gift of salvation. We should go to them with confidence.

---

[18] Solomon and Adonijah both had the same father, King David, but Bathsheba was Solomon's mother, whereas Haggith was the mother of Adonijah (2 Sam. 3:4).

6

"Be Perfect,
as Your Heavenly Father Is Perfect"
(Mt. 5:48)

*Drawing Closer to Christ and Preparing for Heaven
by Celebrating and Living the Sacraments*

As we have seen, Baptism is the gateway to the Christian
life, and the Eucharistic Sacrifice/Mass is the fundamental
way that Jesus Christ nourishes us and deepens our union
with him along our journey to heaven. To aid us further in
conforming ourselves to Christ and giving us access to his
greatest blessings, e.g., eternal salvation (CCC 1129), Jesus
provides us with several other sacraments, which also help
us in giving a joyfully faithful witness so that the harvest
for the kingdom of God may be great (see Mt. 9:37–38).

Sacraments are sensible signs instituted by Christ to convey grace (CCC 1131; see 1114–16). There are seven sacraments in all: Baptism, Eucharist, Confirmation, Confession
or Reconciliation,[1] Holy Orders (including the ministerial
priesthood), Matrimony (marriage) and Anointing of the
Sick (CCC 1113).

The sacraments are made possible, first of all, by the Incarnation—God's becoming man in Jesus Christ—whereas

---

[1] The CCC recognizes these longstanding common terms and formally uses
the term "Sacrament of Penance and Reconciliation" in its presentation.

their saving effectiveness is derived from the Paschal Sacrifice of Christ's Passion, Death, Resurrection, and Ascension (CCC 613; 1085). Because it presents anew Christ's one Sacrifice of Calvary,[2] and is therefore "the source and the summit of the whole Christian life," as we saw in Chapter 4, the celebration of the Eucharistic Sacrifice is the "Sacrament of sacraments," St. Thomas Aquinas affirms, because "all the other sacraments are ordered to it as to their end" (CCC 1211).

Indeed, without the celebration of the Eucharistic Sacrifice, the other sacraments would not be fruitful—*and could not be fruitful* (see CCC 1324; 1067). Without Christ's one atoning Sacrifice, Baptism, Confession and Anointing of the Sick could not forgive sins and promote healing in other ways; there would be no ministerial priesthood, for there could be no Eucharistic Sacrifice to offer; Christ would not have died for his mystical bride, the Church, so human marriage could not be raised to the level of a sacrament; and Confirmation could not complete the process of Christian initiation that Baptism begins.

The Universal Call to Holiness

Whether one is married, single, a priest, a member of a religious community, etc., all Catholics are called to do their

---

[2] The Eucharistic Liturgy or Mass is the action of the Church that *brings* Jesus —namely, his one Paschal Sacrifice—into our presence sacramentally, while the Blessed Sacrament, the chief fruit of the Mass, *is* Christ among us. Together they are the paramount way that Jesus remains with us until he visibly returns at his Second Coming (see Mt. 28:20).

part in advancing the Church's mission to make disciples of all nations (Mt. 28:18–20). The Second Vatican Council reminds us of this "universal call to holiness."[3]

God gives different gifts to different disciples, and so some are called to be apostles (bishops), some evangelists, some pastors and teachers, etc. (Eph. 4:11–12). But all of us who are disciples of Christ are to give joyful witness to the Gospel in our lives, and the sacraments enable us to serve faithfully, especially in healing us of the causes and effects of sin in our lives. As Jesus says, everyone must carry the cross that comes with being a disciple (Mt. 10:37–39; 16:24–26). Yet, if we stay faithful to Christ and his Church, responding to God's graces—particularly as received in the sacraments—we will find again and again the redemptive value of uniting our sufferings with Christ's, with personal "Good Fridays" leading to "Easter Sundays." That is, each person's life has little "Paschal events," recurring opportunities to persevere through suffering to a point of renewed —and deeper—joy and blessing. God will see us through such trials, so that we can say like St. Paul, "I can do all things in him who strengthens me" (Phil. 4:13; see 2 Cor. 12:8–10; Is. 40:31).

And even though we may not be the most skilled in explaining and defending the Church's teachings, all of us can share with others how God has made a difference in our lives, and all of us can invite people—be they struggling or fallen-away Catholics, Protestant Christians, or non-Christians—to spend quiet time before the Eucharistic

---

[3] Vatican II, *Lumen Gentium* (LG), 39ff.; http://www.vatican.va/archive/hist_councils/ii_vatican_council/documents/vat-ii_const_19641121_lumen-gentium_en.html.

Lord in a nearby Catholic church.[4] All Catholics can charitably encourage others to humbly ask Jesus that if he really
exists—and if the Eucharist is what the Catholic Church
claims it is—to please make himself known in their lives in
the days, weeks, months and years going forward. And to
encourage them to repeat this prayer periodically, whether
while visiting a Catholic church again, in the privacy of
their own homes or wherever else. *Great things can and will
happen when we humbly and perseveringly seek Christ the Lord*
(see Mt. 7:7–12).[5]

Sacraments of Initiation

There are three "sacraments of Christian initiation"—Baptism, Eucharist and Confirmation—because they "lay the
foundations of every Christian life" (CCC 1212, emphasis
original). Pope Paul VI adds:

---

[4] For such time of quiet reflection and prayer, the Eucharist could be re-
served in the tabernacle or exposed in a monstrance. See footnote 21 in Chapter 4.

[5] In addition to personal prayers to Jesus and God the Father, other highly
recommended brief prayers include the "Lord's Prayer" or "Our Father" (CCC
2759) and "Come Holy Spirit"; https://www.ewtn.com/faith/teachings/spirb5a
.htm. I also like, "Jesus, I trust in you; help my lack of trust." Intercessory
prayers to the angels and saints are also recommended, particularly to the
Blessed Mother, e.g., the "Hail Mary" (CCC 2676–79) and the "Memorare";
http://ewtn.com/Devotionals/prayers/Memorare.htm. Also, for Christians in
particular, there is the prayer to your guardian angel; http://ewtn.com/Devotion
als/prayers/angel2.htm. Longer prayers to which one can progress include the
Chaplet of Divine Mercy, http://www.thedivinemercy.org/message/devotions/
chaplet.php; and the Rosary, in which one meditates upon key events in the life
of Jesus with the aid of his Blessed Mother (CCC 2708); http://www.usccb.org/pr
ayer-and-worship/prayers-and-devotions/rosaries/how-to-pray-the-rosary.cfm.

> The sharing in the divine nature given to men through the grace of Christ bears a certain likeness to the origin, development, and nourishing of natural life. The faithful are born anew by Baptism, strengthened by the sacrament of Confirmation, and receive in the Eucharist the food of eternal life. By means of these sacraments of Christian initiation, they thus receive in increasing measure the treasures of the divine life and advance toward the perfection of charity (CCC 1212).

In giving his Apostles the Great Commission to "make disciples of all nations," Jesus makes clear that the Church makes disciples by *"baptizing them in the name of the Father and of the Son and of the Holy Spirit,* teaching them to observe all that I have commanded you; and behold I am with you to the close of the age" (Mt. 28:18–20; emphasis added; CCC 1223). Indeed, as we have seen in detail in Chapter 3 and Jesus makes plain just before his Ascension, Baptism is fundamental to discipleship and salvation; and the sacrament is to be conferred in the name of the Triune Godhead or Holy Trinity—i.e., in the name of the Father, the Son and the Holy Spirit (CCC 1240; see CCC 232–34; 253–67).

As we saw in Chapter 4, Jesus institutes the Eucharistic Sacrifice at the Last Supper:

> And he took bread, and when he had given thanks he broke it and gave it to them, saying, "This is my body which is given for you. Do this in remembrance of me." And likewise the cup after supper, saying, "This cup which is poured out for you is the New Covenant in my blood" (Lk. 22:19–20).

In addition, it is only when Jesus ascends to the heavenly sanctuary to culminate his one Sacrifice in everlasting glory (see CCC 659–67), that the Holy Spirit is sent to *fully* inaugurate the Church's mission on the day of Pentecost (see CCC 731–32; 1076). The sacraments are actions of the Holy Spirit (CCC 1116), and we explicitly see Christ empowering his apostles with the Spirit to forgive sins after he rises from the dead (Jn. 20:21–23). In addition, while traveling with two disciples on the road to Emmaus, Jesus celebrates the Eucharistic Sacrifice on Easter Sunday (CCC 1347; Lk. 24:28–35).

Confirmation provides "the completion of baptismal grace" (CCC 1285; see 1304). "Baptism is concerned with the salvation of the individual," Fr. Peter Stravinskas summarizes. "Confirmation takes that saved individual and turns him outward with concern for the salvation of the world."[6]

Like Baptism, Confirmation is received only once, and is conferred by the minister's laying hands on a person's head while praying, "Be sealed with the Gift of the Holy Spirit" (CCC 1300).[7] For "cradle Catholics" in the Latin or Roman Rite, this sacrament is often received in the United States around the eighth grade, although a number of bishops are moving its celebration to a younger age, before the reception of First Holy Communion, i.e., one's initial partaking

---

[6] Fr. Peter M. J. Stravinskas with Henry Dietrich, *Understanding the Sacraments: A Guide for Prayer and Study* (Ann Arbor, MI: Servant Publications, 1984), 78. As I discussed in Chapter 3, and as Fr. Stravinskas would affirm, being saved is not a one-time, irrevocable experience. That is, one can speak of a baptized Christian's being "saved" without implying that he or she is guaranteed a place in heaven. One must persevere in God's gift of salvation.

[7] In the Latin or Roman Rite, Confirmation is conferred ordinarily by a bishop, though for a grave reason a bishop may designate a priest to celebrate the sacrament (see CCC 1312–14).

of the Eucharist (CCC 1307).[8] Confirmation provides "the special outpouring of the Holy Spirit as once granted to the apostles on the day of Pentecost" (CCC 1302; see Acts 2:1–4, 5–42).

The impact of Confirmation is great for those who are well-prepared and open to the leading of the Spirit. Here we are reminded that grace is received according to the disposition of the receiver. In other words, God respects our free will in receiving his grace. The more we accept and cooperate with the gifts of his grace, the more we benefit from them. (In contrast, because the sacraments are *not* magic, *Catholics who resist God's grace can unfortunately become stumbling blocks to non-Catholics who don't see the fruit of the sacraments being borne in their lives, and consequently are less likely to become Catholic. The same holds true for Catholics who don't serve as good role models for their children and/or other young people under their sphere of influence.*[9])

---

[8] The Archdiocese of Denver is an example, stating that "the standard age of Confirmation is going to be lowered to third grade, and Confirmation will be given before, not after, First Communion. *This practice restores Confirmation to its original place*" (emphasis added). Implementation of the restored order can take place "anytime over a three-year period between the Fall of 2017 and the Spring of 2020." For more, see http://saintsdenver.com/.

As the Archdiocese conveys, the change conforms to the *Catechism of the Catholic Church*, which provides, "The holy Eucharist *completes* Christian initiation. Those who have been raised to the dignity of the royal priesthood by Baptism and configured more deeply to Christ by Confirmation participate with the whole community in the Lord's own sacrifice by means of the Eucharist" (CCC 1322). At the same time, the Church also permits dioceses to confer Confirmation *after* the reception of First Communion. In the Church's Eastern rites, Baptism, Confirmation and Eucharist are received together by infants shortly after birth, in that order.

[9] Catholics who have failed to be good witness to their children or others

The *Catechism of the Catholic Church* highlights the power of Confirmation and the gifts it provides:

> Confirmation brings an increase and deepening of baptismal grace:
>
> — it roots us more deeply in the divine filiation which makes us cry, "Abba! Father!" (Rom. 8:15);
> — it unites us more firmly to Christ;
> — it increases the gifts of the Holy Spirit in us;
> — it renders our bond with the Church more perfect;
> — it gives us a special strength of the Holy Spirit to spread and defend the faith by word and action as true witnesses of Christ, to confess the name of Christ boldly, and never to be ashamed of the Cross . . . (CCC 1303, some footnotes omitted).

In Confirmation, St. Ambrose[10] affirms that we receive "the spirit of wisdom and understanding, the spirit of right judgment and courage, the spirit of knowledge and reverence, the spirit of holy fear in God's presence. Guard what you have received" (CCC 1303).

Distinguishing Between Baptism and Confirmation in the Bible

St. John the Baptist preached and administered a baptism of repentance, but he prophesied that one would come

---

close to them should never despair. They should go to Confession and renew their faith in God, while also looking for opportunities to share the Good News with their kids or others close to them. If nothing else, they should continue to pray for their loved ones and try to be involved in their lives, even if religion is discussed rarely.

[10] St. Ambrose was the Bishop of Milan, Italy, and the spiritual father of St. Augustine, Bishop of Hippo, Africa, which is located in modern-day Algeria.

after him who would baptize with the Holy Spirit and fire (Mt. 3:11). Jesus is that man, the Lamb of God who takes away the world's sins (Jn. 1:29, 35–36). Though he is sinless, Jesus submits to John's baptism (Mt. 3:15) "to identify with sinners" for whom he will die and thereby "align himself with God's plan," a plan that includes performing "Old Covenant regulations to fulfill and perfect them in the New (Mt. 5:17; cf. Lk. 2:21–28; CCC 536)."[11] Fire symbolizes God and "his purifying judgment," meaning that Christ's Baptism will forgive sins; and by receiving the Holy Spirit we also become adopted into God's family, the Church.[12]

On "the day of Pentecost" (Acts 2:1), the apostles receive Confirmation by the outpouring of the Holy Spirit. We notice, however, that the apostles don't confer Baptism on each other, but they do baptize fellow Jews who ask what they must do to be saved (Acts 2:37–42). (Perhaps Jesus baptized his apostles sometime earlier, between his Resurrection and Ascension; or the apostles could've baptized each other—and other disciples close to the Lord —sometime between Christ's Ascension and the outpouring of the Holy Spirit on Pentecost.) In addition, the apostles don't immediately lay hands on the fledgling Christians to confer Confirmation, but we know they subsequently did as St. Peter and St. John lay hands on believers who previously received Christian Baptism (Acts 8:14–17).

In the Acts of the Apostles, we see Christian Baptism referred to in an abbreviated form—"in the name of the

---

[11] *The Ignatius Catholic Study Bible New Testament* (San Francisco: Ignatius Press, 2010), 12.

[12] Ibid.

Lord Jesus" (Acts 8:16).[13] But, as noted above, there is no doubt that Jesus commissioned his apostles to baptize "in the name of the Father and of the Son and of the Holy Spirit" (Mt. 28:19). This Trinitarian baptismal formula is what the Church has always used to confer Baptism, and this formula was not an issue among the early Reformers. Some later Christians, relatively few in number, have mistakenly taught that one must be baptized in the name of Jesus alone, drawing an erroneous conclusion from Scripture.[14]

In Acts 19:1–7 we see that some disciples, who had only received John's baptism and had never heard of the Holy Spirit, received first Christian Baptism and then, through the laying on of hands, the Sacrament of Confirmation. So while we don't see Jesus explicitly institute Confirmation in the New Testament, we know that he did so from the witness of his apostles, which Scripture documents; and we

---

[13] "A distinction is made in Acts between Baptism, which confers the Spirit in an invisible way (2:38), and the laying on of hands, which calls down the Spirit to manifest his presence in a visible and charismatic way (19:6)," says _The Ignatius Catholic Study Bible New Testament_ (220–21):

> In the interpretive tradition of the Church, the deeper conferral of the Spirit through the imposition of hands is linked with Confirmation, a sacrament that follows Baptism and is integral to the process of Christian initiation. As in this episode, deacons (Philip) can baptize, but it belongs to the bishops (Peter and John) to bestow a fuller measure of the Spirit on the baptized by the laying on of hands (CCC 1288; 1313).

[14] For an affirmation of the Trinitarian baptismal formula in the early Church, see, e.g., the _Didache_ (the "Teaching of the Twelve Apostles"), ch. 7, v. 1, which dates to the later first or early second century; http://www.newadvent.org/fathers /0714.htm. See also St. Justin Martyr's _First Apology_, ch. 61, which dates to the mid-second century; http://www.newadvent.org/fathers/0126.htm.

can also infer that this sacrament encompasses the "power" Jesus tells his disciples they will receive "when the Holy Spirit has come upon you" (Acts 1:8).

"The Sacraments at the Service of Communion:"[15] Holy Orders and Matrimony

While everyone has their particular God-given mission in life, two vocations have sacraments at their foundation: Holy Orders and Matrimony. These vocations serve to promote the salvation of others and—in the process—the salvation of those God calls to these vocations.

There are three degrees of Holy Orders: the episcopate (serving as a bishop); the presbyterate[16] (serving as a ministerial priest); and the diaconate, i.e. serving as a deacon (CCC 1554ff.).[17] The Reformers rejected this sacrament. They cited the words of St. Peter (1 Pet. 2:5), arguing that Scripture testifies only to the priesthood of all believers. As we have seen before, the Catholic response is that it's a both/and, *not* an either/or. Because of Baptism, all Christians are members of the *common priesthood* of the faithful, participating in Christ's mission as priest, prophet and king according to their respective vocations (CCC 1546). But

---

[15] CCC 1533–35.

[16] The Greek *presbyteros* is often translated as "elder" in the New Testament (Jas. 5:14; 1 Tim. 5:17; Tit. 1:5). The English word "priest" is derived from this Greek word.

[17] Ordinarily, the diaconate is a transitional stage on the way to the ministerial priesthood. However others—typically married men—serve in the permanent diaconate (CCC 1571).

some are also called to serve as *ministerial* priests, namely, ordained priests and bishops (CCC 1547).

Jesus ordains his apostles as the first priests of the New Covenant at the Last Supper,[18] commissioning them to offer the New Covenant Passover/Sacrifice of the Mass in "remembrance" of him, as we examined in Chapter 4. The Mass or Sacrifice of the Eucharist was commonly known in the early Church as "the breaking of the bread" (Lk. 24:30–35; Acts 2:42, 46; 20:7, 11).

Around A.D. 110, St. Ignatius of Antioch affirms that the bishops and those they designate (i.e., "the presbyters") offer the Sacrifice of the Eucharist,[19] which Ignatius teaches is "the Flesh of our Savior Jesus Christ, Flesh which suffered for our sins and which the Father, in His goodness, raised up again."[20]

Another early Church writing is the *Didache* (Greek for "Teaching"), which purports to be the "Teaching of the Twelve Apostles" and was written in the later first or early second century. The *Didache* not only teaches that the Mass had become the focus of Lord's Day (Sunday) worship in the early Church, but it also uses the word "sacrifice" a

---

[18] *The Catechism of St. Pius X*, "The Sacrament of Holy Orders," Q. 4; http://www.catholicbook.com/AgredaCD/PiusX/psacr-o.htm. Jesus also ordains his apostles as the first bishops. The episcopate, or office of bishop, is the fullness of the priesthood (CCC 1557). That is, bishops are priests to a greater degree than ordinary priests.

[19] St. Ignatius of Antioch, *Letter to the Smyrnaeans*, ch. 8, sect. 1, As cited in William A. Jurgens, *The Faith of the Early Fathers* (Collegeville, MN: Liturgical Press, 1970), no. 65, 1:25.

[20] Ibid., ch. 7, sect. 1. As cited in Jurgens, *Faith of the Early Fathers*, no. 64, 1:25.

total of four times to describe the nature of the sacramental celebration. For example, the *Didache* provides: "On the Lord's Day . . . gather together, break bread and give thanks, after confessing your transgressions so that your sacrifice may be pure. . . . For this is that which was proclaimed by the Lord: 'In every place and time let there be offered to Me a clean sacrifice . . .' (see Mal. 1:11)."[21]

The early Church clearly teaches that the Eucharist is indeed a Sacrifice involving Christ's Body and Blood, and —like the *Didache*—St. Justin Martyr (circa A.D. 155)[22] and St. Irenaeus (circa A.D. 199)[23] both affirm that the Eucharist fulfills the Old Testament expectation of a sacrifice "among the nations"—or "Gentiles"—by the prophet Malachi (Mal. 1:11).

The ministerial priesthood and the sacrificial nature of the Eucharist have always been taught by the Catholic Church as well as the Orthodox churches (CCC 1399–1400), and only came into serious question with the Reformers. While they maintained some semblance of the Church's celebration of the Eucharist to varying degrees, as discussed in Chapter 4, Martin Luther, Ulrich Zwingli and John Calvin all taught that the Lord's Supper is not in any way a sacrifice, and so there was no need for a ministerial priesthood. In addition, in contrast to the Catholic

---

[21] *Didache*, ch. 14, sect. 1, 3. As cited in Jurgens, *The Faith of the Early Fathers*, no. 8, 1:4.

[22] St. Justin Martyr, *Dialogue with Trypho*, ch. 41. As cited in Jurgens, *Faith of the Early Fathers*, no. 135, 1:60.

[23] St. Irenaeus, *Against Heresies*, bk. 4, ch. 17, sect. 5. As cited in Jurgens, *Faith of the Early Fathers*, no. 232, 1:95.

Church and the Orthodox churches, all three early Reformers taught that Christ did not establish the Sacrament
of Reconciliation, arguing that the faithful can go directly
to Jesus—without the mediation of a ministerial priest—
to have their sins forgiven.[24]

The biblical record, however, affirms the reality of the
Sacrament of Reconciliation (CCC 1461–67). In giving his
disciples the Lord's Prayer, Jesus teaches that _all_ Christians
must forgive the sins _committed against them personally_; and
that God's "forgiving us of our trespasses" will be contin-
gent upon how "we forgive those who trespass against us"
(Mt. 6:12). In marked contrast, Jesus gives the power to
forgive sins _in general_—and the power to retain those sins if
a priest believes someone is not truly contrite—_to a relative
few_, i.e., his apostles, not to every Christian (Jn. 20:21–23;
see 2 Cor. 5:18).[25] In addition the apostles' successors, like
Matthias, carry on this important ministry (see Acts 1:15–
26), and the Church has always taught that Jesus extends
the power to retain and forgive sins to the presbyters or
priestly collaborators (CCC 1461ff.).[26] And the same has
always held true among the Orthodox churches as well.
Only God has the power to forgive sins, but he gives his
New Covenant priests the power to forgive sins in his name

---

[24] Protestants generally recognize only two of the seven sacraments Christ
instituted: Baptism and the Lord's Supper/Eucharist, although, again, they do
not believe in the sacrificial nature of the Eucharist.

[25] The authority to "forgive and retain" sins is contained within the larger
power "to bind and loose" (Mt. 16:19; 18:18; CCC 1443–45), which Jesus gave
to St. Peter and the other apostles (CCC 553; 730).

[26] The term "elder" was also used to describe priests (Jas. 5:14).

(CCC 1441–42). So the ministerial priesthood is another reminder that God has used subordinate human collaborators to carry forth his mission throughout salvation history.

Holy Matrimony:
One in Christ

The other sacrament at the service of "building up the People of God" is Matrimony or marriage (CCC 1534). Marriage is a *natural* institution with which God blesses humanity, beginning with Adam and Eve. But Jesus elevates it to the level of a *sacrament*. In anticipation of doing so, Jesus says that divorce was a concession allowed by Moses for the hardness of the Israelites' hearts, and so is contrary to God's original and enduring plan for marriage (Mt. 19:4–8; see Gen. 2:23–24). Jesus makes an exception for "unchastity" (Mt. 19:9).[27]

Similar to the mystical union between Christ and his Church, a validly ratified and consummated marriage between two Christians cannot be broken, although the latter

---

[27] Matthew 19:9 is known as "the exception clause" regarding *porneia*, Greek for "unchastity." The two most common understandings of the exception clause are the "Patristic View," i.e., held by a number of the early Church Fathers, which says that one may divorce in case of serious sexual sin, but the marriage bond continues so that husband and wife are not free to remarry (see 1 Cor. 7:10–11). The other common view is that *porneia* refers to a marriage between two close blood relatives, i.e., a relationship that was never a valid marriage. This is known as the "Levitical Law View" and is an example of a "declaration of nullity" or annulment. For more on annulments, see Edward Peters, J.D., J.C.D, *Annulments and the Catholic Church: Straight Answers to Tough Questions*, rev. ed. (West Chester, PA: Ascension Press, 2004).

is dissolved by the death of one of the spouses.[28] In Ephesians 5:21–33, St. Paul elaborates on Christian marriage in light of Christ's mystical union with the Church. In modern times, some Christians—particularly women—take great issue with Paul when he teaches that wives should be subject to their husbands in everything, as the Church is subject to Christ (Eph. 5:24).

One should not misunderstand St. Paul's analogy. Christ is perfect, whereas merely human husbands—say it isn't so!—are not. In addition, a husband's being the head or leader of his home certainly does *not* mean that he should be domineering. Rather, a husband should recognize and celebrate his wife as his equal, laying down his life for her and their children. This self-sacrificing love is what St. Paul speaks of in the next verse: "Husbands, love your wives *as Christ loved the Church and gave himself up for her* . . ." (Eph. 5:25, emphasis added). That's a very tall order that is only possible in Christ Jesus, and a wife who knows she is truly loved by her husband will not have a problem accepting his household leadership.

St. Paul also teaches that husbands and wives should be "subject to one another out of reverence for Christ" (Eph. 5:21). In this regard, a line from the old marriage rite should provide *all* spouses food for prayerful reflection, as they live out their vocations in giving faithful witness to each other, their children and the world at large: "Sacrifice is usually difficult and irksome. Only love can make it easy,

---

[28] *The Code of Canon Law*, canon 1141; http://www.vatican.va/archive/ENG11 04/_P44.HTM. See also CCC 1625–32; 1644–45.

and perfect love can make it a joy."[29] In Christ Jesus, such perfect love is possible.

The Sacrament for the Sick

The Sacrament of Anointing of the Sick is the seventh sacrament, and the second "sacrament of healing" along with Confession/Reconciliation (CCC 1420ff.). This sacrament confers a special grace to provide strength, peace and courage "to overcome the difficulties" associated with serious illnesses and the frailty of old age (CCC 1520). Consequently, this sacrament is not only for those who are at the point of death, as is sometimes thought, but for those having a serious operation, e.g., one for which they will be sedated, as well as for those struggling with any serious illness, including clinical depression (see CCC 1514–15).

A person also receives forgiveness of their sins in this sacrament and the grace to unite their sufferings with Christ's (CCC 1520–21; see 1522–23). Jesus prayed over many people during his earthly ministry, and St. James provides biblical testimony that Christ instituted this sacrament of healing: "Is any among you sick? Let him call for the elders of the church, and let them pray over him, anointing him with oil in the name of the Lord; and the prayer of faith will save the sick man, and the Lord will

---

[29] *Rituale Romanum*, 1962 ed., *Rite of Christian Marriage*, "Instruction on the Day of Marriage and Exhortation before Marriage"; http://www.sanctamissa.org/en/resources/books-1962/rituale-romanum/66-matrimony-instruction.html.

raise him up; and if he has committed sins, he will be forgiven" (Jas. 5:14–15; see CCC 1520).[30]

Sick Catholics who are conscious and capable of confessing their sins to a priest—and who also haven't been to Sunday Mass regularly and/or Confession in a long while—should receive the Sacrament of Reconciliation first. So too should any other person who is conscious and also aware of unconfessed mortal sin (see CCC 1532). God will not force his merciful love upon us, nor coerce ours. Rather, he offers it freely and in spite of our unworthiness. On the other hand, for those who are seriously ill and unconscious, the Church faithfully administers the sacrament and commends them to the Good Lord's mercy.

Those who are near death and are properly disposed may also receive viaticum—i.e., consume the Eucharist—to aid them further in transitioning from this world to eternal life (CCC 1524–25).

Purgatory and Indulgences:
Final Aids on the Highway to Heaven

The Reformers uniformly rejected the Church's teaching on Purgatory, that state of final purification prior to one's entrance into heaven (CCC 1030–32). They argued that

---

[30] In his original preface to the Letter of James, as we saw in Chapter 3, Luther says that St. James "names Christ twice" in his epistle "but teaches nothing about him." Yet, we are indebted to James for providing the only scriptural testimony for this sacrament that Jesus instituted, a sacrament which mercifully provides healing, including the forgiveness of sins.

Purgatory contradicts the sufficiency of Christ's Sacrifice and is an outgrowth of an erroneous "works righteousness" view of salvation. One either goes to heaven or hell when they die, they would summarize.

The Catholic Church agrees that there are only two ultimate destinies, as Jesus teaches in the parable of the sheep and goats (Mt. 25:31–46). But for some of the saved —maybe the great majority—heaven *can* wait, as it turns out. And not simply can wait, *but will have to wait.* If we are not fully prepared for communion with the Father, the Son and the Holy Spirit, Purgatory will serve as a painful prelude to Paradise, made necessary because entering the gates of heaven unmistakably requires letting go of *everything* and *everyone* that impedes our reception of God's love (see Lk. 14:26–27).

Consider the words of Jesus. After proclaiming that it profits a man nothing to gain the whole world at the expense of everlasting life with the Lord God (Mt. 16:24–26; Mk. 8:34–38), Christ teaches that we all will have to render an account for how we have lived our lives: "For the Son of man is to come with his angels in the glory of his Father, *and then he will repay every man for what he has done*" (Mt. 16:27, emphasis added; see 12:33–37).

In other words, as we saw in detail in Chapter 3, our life choices or works express whether we accept or reject God's gift of salvation. They *do* make a difference. St. Paul reaffirms the teaching of Jesus, teaching that God "*will render to every man according to his works*: to those who by patience in well-doing seek for glory and honor and immortality, he will give eternal life; but for those who are factious and do not obey the truth, but obey wickedness, there will be wrath and fury" (Rom. 2:6–8, emphasis added; see 2:13–15).[31]

More to the point, *what about our life choices that merit neither eternal life nor eternal condemnation?* What about choices in which we've grown attached to persons or things in an unholy way, while still maintaining our relationship with God? Or what about mortal sins for which we've repented but to which we still have some unholy attachment?

That's what Purgatory is about. Jesus tells the parable of the unmerciful servant (Mt. 18:23–35). He refused to forgive a fellow servant a minor debt after the king had forgiven him an enormous debt—10,000 times 20 years' wages for a laborer (Mt. 18:24).[32] This unmerciful servant is turned over to the jailers or torturers until he pays his debt in full, and Jesus says his heavenly Father will do the same to us unless we forgive others from our heart (Mt. 18:34–35).

Jesus' words about the unmerciful servant imply that not only does he as Lord atone for our sins, but that *we ourselves* must do penance, because sin "has a *double consequence*" (CCC 1472, emphasis original). Sins create a debt of suffering, and this debt must be paid off, even if death comes before we've finished making the payments. And unlike the goats who are condemned to hell for their wrongdoing, the unmerciful servant is told there will be *an end* to his torment or purification, indicating the reality of Purgatory.

---

[31] Romans 2:6–8 seems to be the Pauline biblical trump card that Luther, Calvin, Zwingli, et al., somehow overlooked—or didn't take into account well—in assessing the importance of Christ-centered good works in the life of a disciple.

[32] *The Ignatius Catholic Study Bible New Testament*, 39.

"Burn, Baby, Burn!":[33]
The Redemptive Flame of God's Burning Love

St. Paul provides a brief glimpse into the mystery of Purgatory when he talks about how some Christians who are saved will first pass through a purifying fire that exacts a measure of suffering and loss:

> According to the commission of God given to me, like a skilled master builder I laid a foundation, and another man is building upon it. *Let each man take care how he builds upon it.* For no other foundation can any one lay than that which is laid, which is Jesus Christ. Now if any one builds on the foundation with gold, silver, precious stones, wood, hay, straw —*each man's work will become manifest; for the Day will disclose it, because it will be revealed with fire, and the fire will test what sort of work each one has done.* If the work which any man has built on the foundation survives, he will receive a reward. *If any man's work is burned up, he will suffer loss, though he himself will be saved, but only as through fire* (1 Cor. 3:10–15, emphases added; see 1 Pet. 1:6–7).

Clearly Paul has in view our judgment by God after death (1 Cor. 3:13; see Heb. 9:27). And the man whose work is "burned up" will be saved, but he will first go through a

---

[33] In various small ways, I've sincerely worked to redeem this infamous slogan from the 1960s riots that took place in a number of U.S. cities, including in 1967 in my beloved Detroit, Motown, an event which I recall from my youth. (My family and I were in Canada the day it began—Sunday July 23—and had to take a detour when returning home that evening.) "The Trammps" did their rehabilitative part with their 1970s musical hit "Disco Inferno." And this is my heartfelt—yet theologically lighthearted—attempt to further the cause. Speaking of Motown, I like to say that a Motown concert is the only place you can say without moral reservation, "Lead us unto 'The Temptations.'"

purifying fire so that he will be fit for heaven, for nothing unclean can enter heaven (Rev. 21:27).

Jesus sacrificed his life on the Cross to atone for the *eternal punishment* of our sins. But there is also the *temporal punishment* due our sins, the atonement for which he has designated us to play a part as St. Paul teaches. Jesus' plan of salvation requires that we be "all in," that we personally account for the negative impact our actions have had in this world and on ourselves, and for which we have not done adequate penance. *This includes our need to be purged of unhealthy attachments to ourselves and other persons and things,* so that we can be fit for eternal communion with God (CCC 1472). Indeed, just because we've repented and been absolved of our sins in Confession does not necessarily mean that we are free of all attachment to the related vices. This is the reality of bad habits. In Purgatory, God mercifully purifies us of these unhealthy attachments, so that we will be free to give every ounce of our love and devotion to the Lord.

In their zeal to emphasize God's sovereignty (Calvin) and mercy (Luther), the Reformers forgot the basic reality that real love is a two-way street and thus calls for a response in kind—especially with Jesus who will not simply overwhelm us with his grace irrespective of a genuine free-will response (Calvin), or look the other way regarding our sins (Luther). No, Jesus wants to *truly* rehabilitate us by enabling us to love *as* he does—unconditionally and sacrificially—and Jesus does so through our self-denying and redemptive cooperation. As St. Augustine says so well, "God created us without us: but he did not will to save us without us" (CCC 1847).

Purgatory can be an uncomfortable reminder that salvation is not a one-and-done event, but a lifelong process in which our everyday personal choices definitely have an impact. And this process undoubtedly begins on earth, which is why Jesus emphasizes that we must each bear our cross on our journey to heaven (Mt. 16:24–27).[34]

To aid the faithful departed, our Jewish ancestors offered prayers for the dead (2 Mac. 12:44–46), and it's even possible that, on one occasion, Paul prays for a person who had died (see 2 Tim. 1:16–18).[35] The Church continues this practice by offering Masses for the faithful departed, calling anew on the mercies won by Christ's one Sacrifice of Calvary (CCC 1371).[36] The faithful on earth can also gain indulgences for themselves and for the faithful departed,[37]

---

[34] You might remember—or have heard of—the 1970s hit song "Love Hurts." Though first recorded in the 1960s by both "The Everly Brothers" and Roy Orbison, it was made most famous by a rock band fittingly named "Nazareth." Granted, Nazareth had a more pessimistic take on love in its ballad, but work with me here. All good-natured kidding aside, why else the cross as not only the symbol and the reality of Christ's Sacrifice, but also the *sine qua non*—i.e., something absolutely indispensable—in being his disciple? Jesus repeatedly tells us to pick up our cross if we are to follow him: For "he who does not take his cross and follow me is not worthy of me" and "he who finds his life will lose it, and he who loses his life for my sake will find it" (Mt. 10:38–39; see 2 Cor. 12:8–10). In short, Christian discipleship requires radical trust in Jesus, trust that if we really lose ourselves for his sake he will bless us with unfathomably abundant love (see Jn. 10:10).

[35] *The Ignatius Catholic Study Bible New Testament*, 398.

[36] Our informal prayers can also be offered for the dead. St. Cyril of Jerusalem, among other early Church Fathers, matter-of-factly teaches about the reality of Purgatory and efficacy of related prayers for the dead in his *Catechetical Lectures*, 23 ("On the Mysteries," V.), sects. 9–10.; http://www.newadvent.org/fathers/310 123.htm.

[37] The faithful departed would include anyone who has died in a state of grace, whether formally and visibly Catholic or not. Since we don't know the

drawing on the treasury of satisfactions of Christ and his saints through Christian good works which the Church designates (CCC 1471). Indulgences are not "get out of jail/Purgatory free" cards, as if a person can willfully sin as they wish provided they do certain prescribed good works and prayers. This is a caricature of the doctrine. Indulgences release us from the temporal punishment of *already forgiven sins*. So to benefit from an indulgence, one must have repented of their sins and thus be properly disposed toward God and their fellow man (see CCC 1471–73).

Indulgences are rooted in the power Jesus gave to his Church to bind and loose (Mt. 16:18–19; 18:15–18). This power extends not only to absolving a person of their sins, but also to mercifully freeing them of the aftereffects of sin (see CCC 553). Indulgences are either partial or plenary, remitting some (partial) or the complete (plenary) temporal punishment due to one's sins, including, again, that associated with our unhealthy attachments to ourselves, other persons and things—attachments which *necessarily cannot exist* in heaven (see Rev. 21:27). We can't enter heaven *on our own terms*, and God will not us rid of these attachments without our docile cooperation.

Protestant Christians strongly disagree with the Church's doctrine on indulgences. Yet, for example, those Christians who espouse once saved/always saved also espouse—in effect—the greatest plenary indulgence. No matter what they

---

state of any person's soul when they die, we can commend them to the mercy of God, who knows and judges everyone perfectly. God will apply any indulgences gained to those who have died *and* who can benefit from them, or to someone else in need (see CCC 846–48.)

do after being saved, they believe that not only will all of their sins be forgiven, but they will also be guaranteed the pain-free removal of any attachment to sin that still exists after they die, because they believe there is no Purgatory to remove it otherwise. And any other Protestant who doesn't believe in Purgatory would also necessarily espouse the pain-free, postmortem removal of attachment to any sin.

To gain a plenary indulgence for oneself or a member of the faithful departed, one must receive the Eucharist, go to Confession—thus affirming the need for true repentance —pray for the Pope's intentions, be free of any attachment even to venial sin, and do the required good work associated with the indulgence. The work could be, e.g., the pious reading of Scripture for at least a half hour, praying the Rosary in a group or making a pilgrimage to a designated church.

In short, indulgences are another merciful gift from God to aid us, our friends and family, and the faithful departed in general on the highway to heaven. *Even* our enemies here on earth, for whom we should pray (Mt. 5:43–48), can undergo dramatic changes with Christ's lavish mercy, and then extend that same mercy to others. Catholics should take advantage of *all* of these divine gifts, particularly the sacraments, so that they might navigate that heavenly highway successfully—and help others to do the same.

7

"To Whom Shall We Go?"

(Jn. 6:68)

*Jesus has Given His Catholic Church
the Words and Mission of Eternal Life*

As we observed in Chapter 4, many of Jesus' disciples no longer followed him after his "hard saying" about the Eucharist (Jn. 6:60, 66). Recall that Jesus makes no effort to summon back those disciples who refuse to accept his difficult teaching in John 6, and you would expect a correction or an attempt at clarification if the whole thing was a big misunderstanding, with the crowds taking literally what Jesus only intended figuratively. There *was* an ancient Hebrew idiom about eating flesh, a figure of speech, but we saw that applying it in John 6 renders Christ's words nonsensical: "He who eats my flesh and drinks my blood has eternal life, and I will raise him up at the last day" (Jn. 6:54) is the equivalent of saying, "He who kills me or slanders me has eternal life, and I will raise him up at the last day."

So if you want to do justice to the biblical text in John 6, as we examined, you must understand the idiom as the Jews of Jesus' day used it, *not* like many modern-day Christians, who think that eating Christ's Flesh and drinking his Blood simply means to "consume" his words and thus

179

follow his teaching in general. If that were the case, Jesus' words wouldn't be a hard saying. And the many disciples who left following Jesus' Bread of Life Discourse in John 6 would have stayed.

What *is* hard and requires real trust is believing that Jesus *is* the Passover Lamb of the New Covenant, who not only offers himself in Sacrifice for us (1 Cor. 5:7), but also bids us to eat his Body and drink his Blood to gain eternal life (Jn. 6:52–58). Like the Passover of old, yet far surpassing it, the Eucharist is a communion sacrifice,[1] enabled by the *solitary* shedding of the Lamb of God's blood on Calvary, a sacrificial event that is sacramentally re-presented in each Eucharist; and then (as with the old), always followed by a celebratory banquet for the worshippers—though one with emancipatory implications of eternal importance, not simply ephemeral considerations.

As we also saw in Chapter 4, there is an intimate and inextricable connection between Christ's one Paschal Sacrifice—his Passion, Death, Resurrection and Ascension—and its sacramental re-presentation in the Eucharistic Sacrifice of the Mass. And *that's* why the Mass is truly "the source and the summit of the Christian life:"[2] the *source* because the Mass enables us to offer anew and partake of Jesus' one redemptive Sacrifice, and the *summit* because it's a foretaste of "the marriage supper of the Lamb" (Rev. 19:9), of our incomparable heavenly communion with the Father, Son and Holy Spirit in everlasting glory!

---

[1] Like the Old Covenant Passover, the Eucharist is a type of communion sacrifice. Because Christ is both divine priest and victim, I capitalize the term "Communion Sacrifice" when simply referring to his one Eucharistic Sacrifice.

[2] CCC 1324.

We also observed that the Jewish leaders see Jesus as a false prophet, one whom they view as teaching his fellow Jews to violate an Old Covenant proscription against drinking blood; and that's a key reason why they seek to kill him (Jn. 7:1). So, if you were a Jew at that time, following Jesus *after* he proclaims his teaching on the Eucharist *would be hard*. It became dangerous to be a disciple of Christ after the Bread of Life Discourse. Instead of seeking out his departed disciples, Jesus simply turns to his apostles and asks whether they will leave too.

Peter's reply rings down the corridors of salvation history: "Lord, to whom shall we go? You have the words of eternal life; and we have believed, and have come to know, that you are the Holy One of God" (Jn. 6:68–69). Part of "consuming" Jesus' words of eternal life, of being his faithful disciples, would entail truly eating his Body and drinking his Blood to attain eternal life. That was a hard saying in Jesus' time, and it's a hard saying today, not only because of the opposition many Christians have to such an understanding, but also because of an increasingly secular culture where basic belief in God is less common and often mocked, and even more so belief in miracles like the Eucharist that elude our senses[3] and thus require much more faith.

Nevertheless, Jesus *further* affirms this literal understanding of the Eucharist on the day he rises from the dead, while traveling on the road to Emmaus with two disciples who don't immediately recognize Christ in his glorified bodily

---

[3] However, the lives of the saints personify the wondrous *impact* of regularly receiving the Eucharist, and there are *some* Eucharistic miracles that *sensibly* affirm Church teaching (see http://therealpresence.org/eucharst/mir/a3.html).

state. Their eyes are only "opened"[4] when Jesus engages in "the breaking of the bread," an early-Church term for the celebration of the Eucharistic Sacrifice (Lk. 24:28–35; see Acts 2:42). Jesus mysteriously vanishes when his two disciples recognize him. Christ withdraws his visible presence because he now remains with his disciples in the Eucharistic meal. It is thus implied that the manner of Jesus' presence amidst his followers undergoes a transition from the clearly "visible" to the "sacramental" (CCC 1329). This Real Presence will require more faith, and it will also be the paramount way Jesus fulfills his words to always be with his Church until his Second Coming (Mt. 28:20; see Lk. 22:19–20).

Chafing at Being Childlike:
Anti-Catholicism and the Strangest of Bedfellows

Because of hard sayings like his teaching on the Eucharist, and because of his call to repent, die to ourselves and radically trust in him, Jesus Christ and his Catholic Church are often opposed by unbelievers. Jesus tells us that we must become like little children[5] to inherit the kingdom

---

[4] The eyes of the disciples on the road to Emmaus were opened to the reality of eternal life, in contrast to Adam and Eve, whose eyes were "opened" to sin, shame and death when they transgressed against God in the Garden of Eden (Gen. 3:7).

[5] Being _childlike_ is definitely not the same as being _childish_. The latter evinces the immaturity that often goes with childhood. The former bespeaks the radical trust children can often exhibit toward their parents, a trust in God which needs to continue in adulthood and which admittedly can be difficult. The world chafes at being childlike precisely because of the radical trust and death to self it requires.

of God (Mt. 18:1–4; 19:13–15), and he has charged the Church to be his prophetic voice in the world (see Mt. 28:18–20; 16:18–19), to advance a mission which is often at odds with various social forces, whose own *self-appointed* missions seriously clash with the Gospel.

In short, there are certain individuals, groups and enterprises that especially chafe in hearing the Gospel message. They refuse faith in Christ and his Church—to one extent or another—because of one or more factors, such as pride, self-centeredness, dislike of authority and moral demands, idolization of progress over tradition and truth, etc. For example, they realize that they need to sacrifice to gain something or someone worthwhile in their lives. But they *don't* want to be told *how* to sacrifice. *They'll* determine what works for them in the realm of sacrifice and

---

Jesus leads the way in modeling childlikeness, asking his Father in heaven *three times* to take away his cup of suffering during his Agony in the Garden of Gethsemane, yet always saying submitting his human will to the divine will (Mt. 26:37–44). And so while Jesus appears to be at his ignominiously weakest during his Passion and Death, these events paradoxically become the occasion of his greatest triumph—and ultimately *our* greatest triumph (see 2 Cor. 12:8–10).

So too the Blessed Mother, that disciple par excellence and thus the epitome of childlikeness. Her "Fiat," her "Behold the handmaid of the Lord: Be it done to me according to thy word," serves as a primary and indispensable example of being childlike (Lk. 1:38, emphasis added; traditional "Angelus" prayer rendering). The abundant fruit of learning and living this lesson is writ large in the lives of the Blessed Mother and all of the other saints. And I would include my little sister Mary, who had Down Syndrome, in their number. For the remembrance I gave at her funeral Mass, see "Shaming the Wise and the Strong: Remembering My Little Sister Mary," *National Catholic Register*, February 24, 2017; http://www.ncregister.com/blog/tom-nash/shaming-the-wise-and-the-strong.

self-denial, thank you very much. Yet, Jesus has the audacity to say otherwise. And because he is "the way, and the truth, and the life" (Jn. 14:6), we should all listen.

So because the full Gospel message is not always welcome, and because Jesus has entrusted his Gospel mission to his Catholic Church, when the Church consistently proclaims the call to repent and reform, various social forces can and do array to silence the Church's prophetic voice.

As a result, even the worst enemies can find common cause in energetically opposing the Church. In fact, I would argue that organizations, enterprises and individuals who marshal their efforts against the Catholic Church, while often differing sharply in their ideologies and aims, sometimes make for the strangest of bedfellows. To be clear, not in a formal alliance. But in an unexpected joint purpose.

For example, Adolf Hitler and Joseph Stalin were mortal enemies during World War II (WWII), but both sought to discredit and destroy the Church—Hitler and his Nazi colleagues particularly during WWII,[6] and then Stalin extending beyond the war, with his Soviet-Communist successors continuing in the decades following.[7]

---

[6] See Catholics United for the Faith (CUF) Faith Fact "Pius XII and the Jews"; http://www.cuf.org/2004/04/friend-in-word-and-deed-pius-xii-and-the-jews/. See also Ronald J. Rychlak, *Hitler, The War, and the Pope*, rev. and expand. ed. (Huntington, IN: Our Sunday Visitor, 2010); and Rychlak, *Righteous Gentiles: How Pius XII and the Catholic Church Saved Half a Million Jews from the Nazis* (Dallas: Spence Publishing Co., 2005). See also Mark Riebling, *Church of Spies: The Pope's Secret War Against Hitler* (New York: Basic Books, 2015).

[7] See in particular Lt. Gen. Ion Mihai Pacepa and Ronald J. Rychlak, *Disinformation: Former Spy Chief Reveals Secret Strategies for Undermining Freedom, Attacking Religion, and Promoting Terrorism* (Washington, DC: WND Books, 2013).

Also ardently lining up against the Church and her mission include Planned Parenthood,[8] homosexual advocacy groups like the Human Rights Campaign,[9] the American Civil Liberties Union (ACLU)[10] and militant atheists like Richard Dawkins and Bill Maher.[11]

Then there are more radical Protestant Christian entities like Bob Jones University, whose chancellor, upon the

---

[8] Planned Parenthood is a leading provider of abortion in America and around the world through the International Planned Parenthood Federation. Margaret Sanger, Planned Parenthood's founder, was a prominent eugenicist in the twentieth century and worked to promote sterilization and other contraceptive measures against those groups she deemed "unfit." See Robert Marshall and Charles Donovan, *Blessed Are the Barren: The Social Policy of Planned Parenthood* (San Francisco: Ignatius Press, 1991). Among other resources, Marshall and Donovan accessed the Sophie Smith Collection at Smith College, which contains a large number of papers of both Margaret Sanger and the Planned Parenthood Federation of America. One of Sanger's endeavors was the infamous "Negro Project," aimed at regulating the reproductive practices of African-Americans.

[9] For anyone dealing with same-sex attraction issues, I highly recommend the resources of the Catholic apostolate Courage (https://couragerc.org/), including their powerful documentary "Desire of the Everlasting Hills" (https://everlasting hills.org/movie/).

[10] The ACLU was more principled in its defense of religious liberty in decades past, e.g., not interfering with the rights of Catholic hospitals to provide authentic health care. Unfortunately, that hasn't been the case in more recent years. See Dr. Grazie Pozo, "ACLU's War on Catholic Hospitals Continues," *The Detroit News*, November 2, 2016; http://www.detroitnews.com/story/opinion/2016/11/02/aclu-catholic-hospital-christie/93221388/.

[11] Maher told CNN's Piers Morgan that he agrees with Richard Dawkins: On a scale of one to seven, with one being absolutely certain that there is a God and seven being absolutely certain that there is no God, he's a 6.9, because "we just don't know." Maher also described himself as an "apatheist," a term combining apathy and atheism: "I don't know what happens when you die," summarized Maher, "and I don't care. No one is ever gonna know"; http://religion.blogs.cnn.com/2011/07/12/maher-on-religion/

death of the pontiff in August 1978 said, "Pope Paul VI, archpriest of Satan, a deceiver and an antichrist, has, like Judas, gone to his own place."[12] And the Ku Klux Klan (KKK), which has always ostracized Catholics along with blacks and Jews. And also radical Islamic groups like ISIS, which seek the destruction of the Catholic Church.[13]

While Planned Parenthood, the Human Rights Campaign, the ACLU and militant atheists like Dawkins and

---

[12] As one who began following the news at a young age beginning in the late 1960s, I clearly remember reading an article in _The Ann Arbor News_ in the late 1970s when Bob Jones, Jr., made this statement. See also Fr. Dwight Longenecker, "American Anti-Catholicism," _Crisis Magazine_, November 28, 2008; http://www.crisismagazine.com/2008/american-anti-catholicism. The future Catholic priest was ironically a student at Bob Jones University when Jones made his infamous comment about Paul VI. The university has never repudiated the statement, nor has it changed its basic theological disposition toward the papacy and the Catholic Church in general. For a helpful Catholic biblical response to the view that the Catholic Church is a tool of Satan, see the chapter on "Peter and the Papacy" in Karl Keating's _Catholicism and Fundamentalism_ (San Francisco: Ignatius Press, 1988). See also the Catholic Answers tracts "The Whore of Babylon"; https://www.catholic.com/tract/the-whore-of-babylon; "Hunting the Whore of Babylon"; https://www.catholic.com/tract/hunting-the-whore-of-babylon; and "Peter and the Papacy"; https://www.catholic.com/tract/peter-and-the-papacy.

[13] See Jay Reed, "Has ISIS Set Its Sights on Occupying The Vatican?" _Newsweek_, March 12, 2016; http://www.newsweek.com/vatican-isis-pope-terrorist-st-peters-obelisk-swiss-guards-papa-paolo-435714. As Reed writes, "ISIS often airs its threats to conquer Rome and convert St. Peter's into a mosque. . . . These aspirations go all the way back to the early years of Islam, when Constantinople—capital of the Eastern Roman empire and bulwark of Christianity in the eastern Mediterranean and West Asia—was an early target of Arab ambitions, although it was only finally conquered for Islam by the Ottoman Turks in 1453." See also Jack Moore, "Italy Uncovers Islamist Plot to Attack Vatican and Israeli Embassy," _Newsweek_, April 28, 2016; http://www.newsweek.com/italy-uncovers-islamist-plot-attack-vatican-and-israeli-embassy-453515.

Maher would basically see each other as allies, they sharply oppose entities like Bob Jones University,[14] the KKK and ISIS. And Bob Jones University, the Klan and ISIS would respond, "Same here," while seeing irreconcilable differences amongst themselves. (Some might counter that Bob Jones University and the KKK have had significant common ground in the university's segregationist past and still have some theological commonalities, particularly regarding their disposition toward the Catholic Church. However, Bob Jones University began parting company with the Klan by admitting its first black student in the early 1970s, then in ending its ban on interracial dating in 2000, and finally by formally repudiating its racist past in 2008.)[15]

And while none of these varying liberal and conservative entities and individuals would want to be grouped with Hitler and Stalin, the two former dictators would have been happy to exclude each of them as well. (Modern militant atheists have had disbelieving common ground with the Soviets,[16] but Dawkins, Maher, etc., strenuously oppose all Communist regimes because of their systematic violation

---

[14] Most Protestant Christians recognize Catholics as fellow Christians, despite some disagreements on key doctrines. As can be inferred from Bob Jones, Jr.'s comment about Pope Paul VI, however, Bob Jones University unfortunately disagrees.

[15] "Bob Jones University Apologizes for Its Racist Past," *The Journal of Blacks in Higher Education*; http://www.jbhe.com/news_views/62_bobjones.html. See also the University's "Statement About Race at BJU"; http://www.bju.edu/about/what-we-believe/race-statement.php.

[16] For an interesting perspective on atheism, see Paul Vitz, *Faith of the Fatherless: The Psychology of Atheism* (Dallas: Spence Publishing Company, 1999). Ignatius Press, based in San Francisco, published a 2nd edition of Vitz's book in 2013.

of basic civil rights.) And yet all of these groups, individuals and enterprises have found common ground—even if for differing yet often overlapping reasons—in zealously opposing the Catholic Church.[17] See if you can find such an eclectic group finding substantive common ground on another important issue. I doubt it.

More to the point, their uniform opposition to the Catholic Church might actually indicate something good about the Church. As Jesus says, "Woe to you, when all men speak well of you, for so their fathers did to the false prophets" (Lk. 6:26). And also, "Blessed are you when men revile you and persecute you and utter all kinds of evil against you falsely on my account. Rejoice and be glad, for your reward is great in heaven, for so men persecuted the prophets who were before you" (Mt. 5:11–12).

All of these various groups and individuals would take great exception to the claim that their opposition to the Catholic Church is an unholy one. Some of them believe in a real devil, while others would acknowledge the existence of evil but not a personal agent and figurehead of evil, such as Satan. In any event, each would argue that they oppose the Church because of *the Church's* evil teachings and practices.

---

[17] You could also add the mainstream secular media, various political groups and a host of other entities which, even if you wouldn't categorize them as anti-Catholic, all strongly oppose the Church's moral teaching on various matters, particularly those related to marriage and family.

The Devil Knows His Real Enemy

And yet, if you asked Satan himself, speaking of unexpected strange bedfellows, he might tell you in a moment of honesty that the Catholic Church is *his* greatest enemy, precisely because the Church is Christ's mystical bride, the new and fulfilled Israel through which the Lord advances his mission to save the world. Which is diametrically opposed to the devil's mission to see all of humanity eternally lost.[18] Satan understands that everlasting life is much more consequential than "four more years," bicentennials or other earthly accomplishments that don't necessarily have eternal implications associated with them. And that should give all of these individuals, groups and enterprises some pause.

There's a reason the devil's disciples call it a "Black Mass." Satan's followers never venture into a Protestant church to steal ordinary grape juice and bread. They always look for Christ himself (see 1 Cor. 11:23–32), which is why they seek out the Eucharist from Catholic churches: So they can desecrate his Real Presence in their rituals.

While they perversely express their acknowledgment of the Almighty, Satanists oddly have more belief in the sacramental "Real Thing" than do many Christians. And those Christians sadly include a good number of Catholics

---

[18] The devil and his infernal underlings were the first who chafed at being childlike, and they did so irrevocably. They now seek to entice a multitude of men and women into joining their everlasting rebellion (see CCC 413–15; 391–95).

who were poorly formed in their faith and/or no longer believe in the reality of the Real Presence. To be sure, Satanists are sworn enemies of the Gospel, whereas Catholics and other Christians who don't recognize the Real Presence are disciples of Jesus to one extent or another. However, because "at the name of Jesus every knee should bow" (Phil. 2:10), the "father of lies" (Jn. 8:44) can't help himself in testifying to Jesus the Eucharistic Lord in a Black Mass, and so some people can ironically and providentially come to know Christ—or know him better—through the blasphemous actions of the devil and his demonic associates (see Rom. 8:28; Jas. 2:19).

Indeed, as we see in Jesus' earthly ministry, demons get a sense of Christ's importance before many of his disciples do (see Mt. 8:28–29; Lk. 4:41). And there's thus a reason why the Catholic Church has a formal Rite of Exorcism and has been engaging in exorcisms since the time of Jesus. Jesus gave his apostles and other disciples the power to exorcise demons (Lk. 9:1; 10:1, 17–20), and the Church has exercised this important ministry ever since.

So Satan knows who his chief enemy is, and the Catholic Church understands that its real enemies are not aforementioned human adversaries like Hitler, Planned Parenthood and ISIS, but Satan and his fallen angelic minions, which include principalities, powers and rulers. St. Paul writes, "For we are not contending against flesh and blood, but against the principalities, against the powers, against the world rulers of this present darkness, against the spiritual hosts of wickedness in the heavenly places" (Eph. 6:12).

Jesus Wants Me to Become A Catholic?!: Keeping Your Eyes on the Church's Divine Founder When His Disciples Falter

When the Catholic Church proclaims that Jesus wants us to make disciples of all nations (Mt. 28:18–20), i.e., invite them to become Catholics, many Protestant Christians[19] and other non-Catholics recoil. As noted in the Preface, and reaffirmed at the start of this chapter, people can balk at becoming Catholic because of Jesus' hard teachings and how those teachings might require them to seriously change their lives to one extent or another. In addition, when you have had 2,000 years of history and your membership is made up of fallen human beings, stumbling blocks can arise from *within* the Church as well.

Speaking of sin, there are a number of events that critics often raise about the Church, and we'll briefly consider several of the more prominent ones. In each case, as with Old Covenant Israel, the sins of New Covenant Church leaders and other Catholics do not nullify the Church's divine foundation and supernatural mission. Making such an assertion does not take lightly misdeeds done in the name of the Church, but rather is said to encourage people, including existing Catholics, not to let the sins of any

---

[19] Many Protestant Christians have been taught that the Catholic Church is a deviant form of Christianity or even, from the perspective of institutions like Bob Jones University, a counterfeit one, as noted. Their opposition to the Catholic Church is certainly influenced by their being born and educated in a religious milieu that is a product of the Reformation.

Catholics prevent you from encountering the Church's divine founder—Jesus Christ—in the full communion of his Catholic Church.

The failings of individual Catholics, including Popes and other ecclesiastical representatives of the Catholic Church, undoubtedly undermine *the witness* of the Church. But they do not undermine *the validity* of her divinely provided mission and teachings. Of course, sin still has a foothold in the Church. Otherwise, there would be no need for the Sacrament of Reconciliation.

In addition, some of these events criticized in Church history have been significantly distorted over time. Take, for example, the case of Galileo in the 1600s, often cited as evidence that the Church is anti-science. A closer look reveals that Galileo was able to make his conclusions precisely because the Church financed his scientific investigations.[20] If Galileo had had the humility of his Catholic predecessor Nicholas Copernicus—who had earlier theorized that the earth revolves around the sun in our solar system and not vice versa[21]—perhaps he wouldn't have endured his trial and subsequent house arrest. This is certainly not to deny that Church officials could have conducted themselves better, but to recognize that Galileo's desire to pronounce on matters both scientific and theo-

---

[20] The Church also developed the scientific method through her great universities.

[21] Copernicanism or heliocentrism teaches that the earth and other planets in our solar system revolve around the sun. This view was not novel to Galileo; Copernicus had proposed it in the previous century. The traditional view was geocentrism, that the sun and other planets revolve around the earth. During the lives of Copernicus and Galileo, heliocentrism was only a theory.

logical[22]—and the acerbic manner in which he chose to do so—undeniably didn't help him and his cause.

As Cardinal Cesare Baronius aptly quipped at the time, in inspiring sacred Scripture "the Holy Spirit's intention is to teach us how to go to heaven, and not how the heavens go."[23] In other words, the Bible was never intended to be a science manual, including making pronouncements on the workings of our solar system. Still, many people think that the Church didn't get it right on the Galileo affair until Pope St. John Paul II issued an apology in 1992. As *The New York Times* correctly noted at the time—although you wouldn't know it by the article's headline and lead paragraphs—the Church removed Galileo's related book from the Index of Forbidden Books as far back as 1757.[24] What

---

[22] Galileo insisted the prevailing scientific view of the world at the time—that the earth was the center of the universe—was mistaken. This was also the prevailing interpretation of the Bible. (This biblical interpretation was never an official Church teaching, nor could it be, as it relates only to science and therefore doesn't deny God as the creator of the universe. But it was the prevailing interpretation at the time, based on inadequate science and some incorrect inferences about Scripture.) Galileo did not dispute the inerrancy of Scripture, but he did note that both St. Augustine and St. Thomas Aquinas taught that the biblical writers did not intend to teach astronomy. Galileo was ultimately proven right, anticipating Pope Leo XIII's 1893 encyclical on scriptural exegesis *Providentissimus Deus*, which notes that the Bible often makes use of figurative language and is not meant to teach science. But in the short term Galileo's zeal was seen by some as calling into question the authority of Scripture.

[23] See Bishop Edoardo Aldo Cerrato, C.O., "How to Go to Heaven, and Not How the Heavens Go"; http://www.oratoriosanfilippo.org/galileo-baronio-english.pdf.

[24] Alan Cowell, "After 350 Years, Vatican Says Galileo Was Right: It Moves," *The New York Times*, October 31, 1992; http://www.nytimes.com/1992/10/31/world/after-350-years-vatican-says-galileo-was-right-it-moves.html.

the *Times* didn't note is that a book teaching Copernican-ism as proven reality and not a theory received an impri-matur in 1822.[25] Three years later in 1825, the Church officially apologized for its condemnation of Galileo, more than 165 years before St. John Paul II's actions.[26]

The Crusades represent another common criticism of the Church. While some reprehensible things took place during the Crusades, such as the sack of Constantinople in 1204, the Church initiated the Crusades in 1095 as a morally legitimate *defensive measure* after centuries of Muslim im-perialism in the Middle East, including atrocities against Christian pilgrims traveling to the Holy Land. Given Mus-lim designs not only to conquer the Middle East but all of Europe, the Church's *resistance* continued until the Battle of Lepanto in 1571[27] and the Battle of Vienna in 1683.[28]

---

[25] George Sim Johnston, "The Galileo Affair," *Lay Witness*, April 1993; http://www.cuf.org/2010/03/the-galileo-affair/.

[26] Patrick Madrid, *Pope Fiction* (Rancho Santa Fe, CA: Basilica Press, 1999), 188. Johnston and Madrid also refute the myth that Galileo was tortured by the Church under Vatican house arrest. In addition, Galileo actually received a well-furnished apartment overlooking the Vatican Gardens, as well as a per-sonal servant.

[27] See Dr. Thomas F. Madden, "The Real History of the Crusades," *Crisis Mag-azine*, March 19, 2011; http://www.crisismagazine.com/2011/the-real-history-of-the-crusades. See also Madden's "Crusade Myths"; http://www.ignatius in-sight.com/features2005/tmadden_crusademyths_feb05.asp; and "Crusaders and Historians," *First Things*, June 2005; https://www.firstthings.com/article/2005/06/crusaders-and-historians. See also Christopher Check, "The Battle that Saved the Christian West," *Catholic Answers Magazine*, November 10, 2011; https://www.catholic.com/magazine/print-edition/the-battle-that-saved-the-ch ristian-west. See also EWTN's four-part mini-series "The Crusades"; https://ww w.ewtnreligiouscatalogue.com/Home+Page/MULTIMEDIA/EWTN+HOME +VIDEO/All/THE+CRUSADES.axd.

[28] Carrie Gress, "The Warrior-King Who Saved Europe from Islam," *National*

The Inquisition, particularly the Spanish Inquisition,[29] is a third major criticism levied against the Church. Though misdeeds undoubtedly occurred, a team of international scholars reports that torture was rare and only one percent of those tried by the Spanish Inquisition were executed, despite prevailing myths that much worse took place. The scholars also affirm that while witch-burning negatively impacted Europe in the 1500s, particularly in Protestant regions, those places which had trained inquisitors quickly vanquished the hysteria.[30] And though it was not an edict of the Spanish Inquisition, the Spanish monarchy's wholesale expulsion in 1492 of Jewish citizens who wouldn't convert was a serious failure in giving witness to the Gospel.[31]

Catholic Register, May 31, 2016; https://www.ncregister.com/blog/cgress/the-warrior-king-who-saved-europe-from-islam.

[29] Contrary to what some think, the Spanish Inquisition did not target Jews and Muslims per se, but rather Catholics, including converts regarding whom it was alleged had become Catholic for social advancement and yet still practiced their original religious faith, or who had converted for sincere reasons but who had later relapsed to their former faith.

[30] Dr. Thomas F. Madden, "The Real Inquisition: Investigating the Popular Myth," *National Review*, June 18, 2004; http://www.nationalreview.com/article/211193/real-inquisition-thomas-f-madden. See also Maria Colonna and Cat Clark, "The Role of the Inquisition in Europe," *Lay Witness*, March 2000, http://www.cuf.org/2000/03/the-role-of-the-inquisition-in-europe/. See also EWTN's four-part mini-series "The Inquisition"; www.ewtnreligiouscatalogue.com/shop.axd/ProductDetails?edp_no=32670.

[31] In 1492, Jews in Spain were required to convert to Catholicism or be expelled from the country. It's true that Spain was a confessional state, in which religion and citizenship were synonymous and so there could be concerns for treason among those who weren't Catholic, the biggest ultimate fallout from which could possibly be imperiling the eternal salvation of some Catholic citizens. However, the state could have expelled those who were truly fomenting treason vs. having a wholesale expulsion of the Jews. In short, telling all Jewish citizens they needed to convert or be exiled cannot be reconciled with the

More recently, the clerical sexual abuse scandal has rocked the Church around the world, beginning in the latter twentieth century and blowing up in the United States in early 2002. While they certainly recognize and lament the scope of the scandal, Church defenders have argued that the rates of sexual abuse of minors—children and adolescents[32]—have been "slightly higher" among Protestant ministers than Catholic clergy, and "significantly higher" among public school teachers than Catholic clergy and other ministers.[33] Still, the abuse of minors by a small

---

Gospel. One cannot coerce in giving faithful witness to the Gospel, and the kind of conversions the Church gets in those situations aren't genuine and the policy also undermines the Church's mission by breeding resentment that can endure for a long time.

[32] Pedophilia involves the abuse of children, whereas ephebophilia involves the abuse of adolescents. Almost 80 percent of the U.S. clerical sexual abuse cases involved adolescent males. See also "The Nature and Scope of Sexual Abuse of Minors By Catholic Priests and Deacons in the United States 1950-2002: A Research Study Conducted by the John Jay College of Criminal Justice, The City University of New York, February 2004, for the United States Conference of Catholic Bishops"; http://www.usccb.org/issues-and-action/child-and-youth-protection/upload/The-Nature-and-Scope-of-Sexual-Abuse-of-Minors-by-Catholic-Priests-and-Deacons-in-the-United-States-1950-2002.pdf.

[33] "Sexual Abuse in Social Context: Clergy and Other Professionals—A Special Report by the Catholic League for Religious and Civil Rights," February 2004; http://www.catholicleague.org/sexual-abuse-in-social-context-clergy-and-other-professionals/. See also William O'Donohue, Ph.D., Olga Cirlugea, Lorraine Benuto, Ph.D., "Some Key Misunderstandings Regarding the Child Sexual Abuse Scandal and the Catholic Church," April 2012; http://www.catholicleague.org/some-key-misunderstandings-regarding-the-child-sexual-abuse-scandal-and-the-catholic-church/. On the general subject of the clerical sexual abuse scandal within the Church, see Philip F. Lawler, _The Faithful Departed: The Collapse of Boston's Catholic Culture_ (New York: Encounter Books, 2008); and Dr. Paul Thigpen, ed., _Shaken by Scandals: Catholics Speak Out about Priests' Sexual Abuse_ (Cincinnati: Charis Books, 2002).

but significant number of Catholic priests (about four percent),[34] and the failure of many bishops in handling this crisis, was clearly reprehensible and has struck a serious blow to the Church's moral authority in the eyes of the world, given how the credibility of a significant number of Church leaders was undermined.

The scandal has shown a need for deep repentance and renewal in the Church. The Church has done much to foster healing and prevent further problems since 2002, and more still needs to take place. These grave sins against minors were a serious betrayal of the Church's teachings and mission. At its core, no one has a higher view of children or human sexuality than the Catholic Church. Continuing to rediscover and reaffirm the Church's teaching on these matters is fundamental to advancing the Church's mission, including ensuring that such crimes are a thing of the past.[35]

Jesus Remains the Reason

As noted in the Introduction, everything about the Catholic Church is ultimately rooted in Jesus Christ and his actions, whether it's the Church's divine foundation; reverence for the sacraments, especially the Eucharist; respect

---

[34] See Laurie Goodstein, "Two Studies Cite Child Sex Abuse by 4% of Priests," *The New York Times*, February 27, 2004; http://www.nytimes.com/2004/02/27/us/two-studies-cite-child-sex-abuse-by-4-of-priests.html. See also the actual John Jay College of Criminal Justice study for the U.S. Bishops noted in footnote 32 above.

[35] For more on this topic, see the chapter on "Priestly Celibacy Caused the Crisis of Sexual Abuse of Minors: The Myth of Priestly Pedophilia" in Christopher Kaczor's *The Seven Big Myths about the Catholic Church: Distinguishing Fact from Fiction about Catholicism* (San Francisco: Ignatius Press, 2012).

for and obedience to the Pope as the Successor of St. Peter on matters of faith, morals and discipline; honoring and seeking the assistance of the Blessed Mother and other saints; etc. And because of the Church's divine pedigree, even those who have pronounced the Church irrelevant and written her obituary—a pastime now for 2,000 years —are themselves ironically preoccupied with the Church. The comedian Bill Maher, who was raised Catholic, can't stop talking about the Church.[36] In addition, television networks have aired various series that take cheap shots at the Church, including "Nothing Sacred" (ABC), "Father Ted" (BBC), "The Real O'Neals" (ABC) and "The Young Pope" (HBO); and we'll likely be treated to more.

That the Catholic Church remains on the minds of her various critics is a backhanded compliment to the Church's enduring relevance—and a reminder of her divine suste-nance. Or as the Jewish comedian Lenny Bruce used to say, the only "_the_ Church" that exists is the Catholic Church.

Meanwhile, after being vilified as "Hitler's Pope" de-spite his actual wartime record, Pope Pius XII is finally being vindicated—or least acknowledged for some of the good he did—by some of his harshest critics. Yad Vashem, the World Holocaust Remembrance Center in Jerusalem,[37]

---

[36] During his younger years as a comedian when Johnny Carson hosted "The Tonight Show," I do recall a great religious joke Maher delivered in reflecting on how his Jewish heritage (his late mother was Jewish) impacted his Catholic faith while growing up in New Jersey: "We used to go into Confession, and I would bring a lawyer in with me. It's true. 'Bless me Father, for I have sinned. And I think you know Mr. Cohen.'"

[37] http://www.yadvashem.org/.

has updated the text on its panel for the Vatican, conceding now that the Pope's record on aiding the Jewish people during WWII is "a matter of controversy among scholars." Yad Vashem also has clarified that "contrary to what has been reported, this change is not a result of Vatican pressure."[38] More recently, after reading Mark Riebling's *Church of Spies: The Pope's Secret War Against Hitler*, prominent atheist Sam Harris summarized, "A fascinating contribution to the literature on the Holocaust, the history of the papacy, and the life of Pius XII. . . . I feel that we should all apologize to Pius XII for our past slanders!"[39]

Despite Pius XII's being vilified by Nazi leaders, praised by contemporary Jewish leaders and affirmed by the secular media during his pontificate for his various efforts, many in the world were all too ready to embrace Soviet-Communist slanders perpetrated against the pontiff, beginning with Rolf Hochhuth's play *The Deputy*[40] in the early 1960s. Because if you can discredit the Pope, the Church's supreme human leader on earth, then you can discredit the

---

[38] http://www.yadvashem.org/yv/en/pressroom/pressreleases/pr_details.asp?ci d=752#!prettyPhoto. See also the recommended resources above in footnotes 6 and 7.

[39] See https://www.amazon.com/Church-Spies-Pope%C2%92s-Secret-Again st/dp/0465022294. See also William Doino, Jr., "St. Pius XII?: A Pope's Heroic Actions in Time of Crisis," *Lay Witness*, September/October 2007; http://www.cu f.org/2007/09/st-pius-xii-a-popes-herioc-actions-in-time-of-crisis/. Doino is also the author of the extensive "Annotated Bibliography of Works on Pius XII, the Second World War, and the Holocaust," in Joseph Bottum and David G. Dalin, eds., *The Pius War: Responses to the Critics of Pius XII* (Lanham, MD: Lexington Books, 2004), 97–280.

[40] See Pacepa and Rychlak, *Disinformation*.

Catholic Church _in general_ in the eyes of many. It didn't work because it was never true,[41] and the sustained effort is another backhanded compliment that reinforces the Church's perennial importance.

Which returns us squarely to our main focus: Jesus. As noted in the Introduction, the Catholic Church would not exist today if it were merely a human institution. We joyfully invite people to become and remain Catholic because what the Church teaches is true. And that truth is not simply a human reality, but ultimately a divine person—Jesus Christ—God who became man. So we share the Gospel out of love, because we want every human being on the planet to experience the transcendent unity that Jesus and the Father have, and which they share with the world through the Church (see Jn. 17:20–23).[42] There can be no greater unity for humanity than that.

To attain that unity, we need to introduce the world to

---

[41] Upon Pius XII's death in 1958, Golda Meir, then Israel's Minister of Foreign Affairs and later the nation's prime minister, echoed the view of many Jewish leaders when she said, "During the 10 years of Nazi terror, when our people went through the horrors of martyrdom, the Pope raised his voice to condemn the persecutors and to commiserate with their victims. The life of our time has been enriched by a voice which expressed the great moral truths above the tumults of daily conflicts. We grieve over the loss of a great defender of peace." As cited in Dr. Joseph Lichten's monograph _A Question of Judgment: Pius XII and the Jews_, reprinted in _Pius XII and the Holocaust: A Reader_ (New York: The Catholic League for Religious and Civil Rights, 1988), 129. Lichten's monograph was originally published by the National Catholic Welfare Conference in 1963, shortly after the debut of "The Deputy." Lichten served as the director of intercultural affairs for the Anti-Defamation League of B'nai B'rith.

[42] Jesus' prayer takes place during the Last Supper, when he introduces the key means for fostering and maintaining oneness—the Eucharistic Sacrifice (see CCC 1323–27)—which we are to celebrate "in remembrance" of him.

the Incarnate Word, "the Word" who "became flesh and dwelt among us" (Jn. 1:14), the God-man Jesus Christ (Jn. 8:58) who came that we "may have life, and have it abundantly" (Jn. 10:10). In the case of Catholics and other Christians, that'll mean a deeper *reintroduction*. And because the Sacrifice of the Eucharist/Mass is "the source and summit of the Christian life," an important way to do that is to invite Catholics and non-Catholics to encounter —or reencounter—our Eucharistic Lord at Mass. Because non-Catholics and alienated Catholics may not be inclined to come to Mass, I also suggest a less formal, yet still powerful way to encounter Jesus, one which has borne great fruit for centuries: Eucharistic adoration.

I propose that dioceses throughout the United States— and around the world—regularly open their churches beyond their Sunday and daily Mass schedules to both their parishioners and the general public, welcoming everyone to visit and be open to the Eucharistic Jesus. And that they invite Catholics and non-Catholics alike to ask the Lord to show he is real by positively impacting their lives. Parish churches could be opened a couple of nights each week, e.g., on Tuesdays from 5–10 p.m. to accommodate people who might want to come right after work, and from 7–10 p.m. on Thursdays.

Praying before the exposed Blessed Sacrament might be too much for some people, who might not be ready to recognize and adore Jesus as "the bread of life" (Jn. 6:35).[43] So I propose that on Tuesdays our Eucharistic Lord could

---

[43] On the other hand, some non-Catholics and alienated Catholics may be ready to encounter—or reencounter—Jesus via Eucharistic adoration with exposition. The decision can be left to them.

remain within the tabernacle and on Thursdays there could be Eucharistic adoration with exposition, making sure on both days that there is a good deal of quiet time. That way, people will be more likely to come and encounter Christ for the first time—or in a renewed and/or deeper way. And once a month there could be an associated informal parish dinner targeted at reconnecting—and/or connecting on a higher level—Catholic men with Christ and his Church, so that these men can be better equipped to serve as leaders in their families, their parishes and beyond.

Jesus is the New Covenant Passover Lamb. He also fulfills the Day of Atonement sacrifices and he perfects the priesthood according to the order of Melchizedek. We are reminded of this collective and profound reality at every celebration of the Mass, when we offer anew and partake of his one Sacrifice, and are thereby also reminded that Jesus remains with us until he returns in visible glory at the consummation of human history. For now, the Lord dwells among us 24/7 in the tabernacle in the Blessed Sacrament —the chief fruit of every Mass—and Jesus thus fulfills how his heavenly Father [44] made himself most intimately present in the Old Covenant holy of holies. Except now, *everyone* can draw close to have an intimate encounter with the Almighty!

Mother Angelica, the foundress of the Eternal Word Television Network (EWTN), realized the importance of the Eucharist in drawing people to the Church. And so, at the network's Irondale, Alabama, headquarters, she posted a sign of welcome to "the people of all

---

[44] See Mt. 5:17.

faiths,"[45] that they might encounter Jesus in the Blessed Sacrament in Our Lady of the Angels Chapel.[46] The same is true for the Shrine of the Most Blessed Sacrament that Mother built for her religious sisters and herself in nearby Hanceville, Alabama.[47] To aid her efforts in educating both Catholics and non-Catholic visitors to the Shrine, Mother also built the John Paul II Eucharistic Center.[48]

If Catholics truly believe in the supreme importance of the Sacrifice of the Mass and Christ's Real Presence in the tabernacle, then we need to proclaim that loudly in a joyful way. If the heart of evangelization and a deeper life with God is encountering Jesus Christ, then there are no better ways than the Mass and Eucharistic adoration for that encounter to happen, for both Catholics and non-Catholics alike. While Protestant Christians and non-Catholics may not receive the Eucharistic Jesus in the intimacy of Holy Communion,[49] there is no impediment to their spending time in prayerful inquiry with our Eucharistic Lord. In addition, there are other ways they can foster a deep and personal relationship with Jesus, such as personal prayer, acts of Christian charity, reading Scripture, listening to good preaching, and participating in the Church's Rite of Christian Initiation of Adults (RCIA) program. All of these Gospel endeavors can aid a person in encountering

---

[45] http://wikimapia.org/19166406/Our-Lady-of-Angels-Chapel-EWTN#/photo/1589628.

[46] https://s-media-cache-ak0.pinimg.com/originals/40/d7/35/40d7357509cd64a4db3aa3e81162f41c.jpg.

[47] http://olamshrine.org/.

[48] http://olamshrine.org/sites/john-paul-ii-eucharistic-center/.

[49] For exceptions, see *The Code of Canon Law*, canon 844.

Jesus, an encounter which is meant to *culminate* in *regular* sacramental Communion as increasingly more faithful—and thus more committed—disciples.[50]

If we enable people to encounter the God-man, if we allow him to be God in all of his glory so as to facilitate those divine encounters,[51] if we as Catholics give a vibrantly fruitful witness in receiving our Lord in Holy Communion on a regular basis, then we in the Church will be reminded and further convicted that our greatest asset —and the fundamental reason why we and everyone else should be Catholic—is our Eucharistic Lord and mystical spouse, Jesus Christ. And we will be all the more motivated to share the Truth who alone can set the world free (Jn. 14:6; 8:31–32), in the hope that everyone might experience the incomparable peace which only he, the Lord Jesus, can deliver (Jn. 14:27):

> O God, who at our celebration of the feast day of the blessed Apostle Peter have nourished us by communion in the Body and Blood of Christ, grant, we pray, that this redeeming

---

[50] See Sherry A. Weddell, *Forming Intentional Disciples: The Path to Knowing and Following Jesus* (Huntington, IN: Our Sunday Visitor, 2012). Weddell is the co-founder and executive director of the Catherine of Siena Institute, which equips Catholic parishes to form lay disciples; https://siena.org/our-mission. See also Mark Shea, "Five Steps to Becoming an Intentional Disciple: Continuing Conversion Is Necessary for All as We Walk the Road to Christ," *OSV Newsweekly*, August 6, 2014; https://www.osv.com/OSVNewsweekly/ByIssue/Article/TabId/735/ArtMID/13636/ArticleID/15855/5-steps-to-becoming-an-intentional-disciple.aspx.

[51] Various parishes throughout the world are taking advantage of Eucharistic adoration, as are groups like the Fellowship of Catholic University Students (FOCUS). For more information on FOCUS, visit https://www.focus.org/.

exchange may be for us a Sacrament of unity and peace. Through Christ our Lord ("Prayer after Communion," Feast of the Chair of St. Peter the Apostle, February 22).[52]

---

[52] International Commission on the Liturgy (ICEL), *The Roman Missal*, 3rd ed. As cited in *Daily Roman Missal* (Woodridge, IL: Midwest Theological Forum, 2011), 1774.

Appendix

Bodily Present in Heaven *and* in the Blessed Sacrament

The Miracle of the Eucharist

No Christian doubts that Jesus Christ can be everywhere *as a divine Person*. But we understandably struggle more when we try to imagine his *limited* human body in more than one place at one time. If Christ is present in his glorified body in the heavenly sanctuary, ministering as a priest forever, how can he be bodily present anywhere else, since he has only one glorified, albeit finite, body?

The answer goes to the heart of the Eucharistic Mystery, which is often referred to simply as "the mystery par excellence."[1] A divine mystery is a truth that we, humanly speaking, will never be able to comprehend fully. It is a truth so big that we cannot wrap our minds all the way around it. We can grasp it somewhat with our reason, but a divine mystery inevitably transcends—not contradicts—our ability to understand. In addition, we must recognize that the Eucharistic Mystery is an extension of another mystery: the Incarnation, in which the divine Son of God assumed a human nature when Mary conceived him by the power of the Holy Spirit (see CCC 456; 461–63;

---

[1] Matthias Joseph Scheeben, *The Mysteries of Christianity*, trans. Cyril Vollert (St. Louis, MO: B. Herder, 1946), 469. See also the treatment of St. Thomas Aquinas on this issue in Part Three, Question 76 of his *Summa Theologica*.

484–86). His being a divine Person with two natures—one divine and one human—is known as the "hypostatic union" (see CCC 464–69), and this explains why we call Jesus the "God-man."

In his divinity, Christ is omnipotent (all-powerful), omniscient (all-knowing) and omnipresent (everywhere). The *Catechism of the Catholic Church* affirms God's and thus Christ's omnipresence (no. 2671), as does Sacred Scripture (Deut. 4:39; Mt. 5:35; 6:9–10; Acts 17:24–28). In his divine essence, Jesus is a pure spirit. He is wholly present in an undivided manner everywhere. In his divine essence, therefore, Jesus has no parts, although he did take on a human nature at his Incarnation. By way of comparison, we as human persons are by nature body-soul composites (see CCC 362–68). Our bodies have parts but our souls, as created spirits, do not have parts. Thus, each person's soul animates (enlivens) his body and is present throughout his body in a whole and undivided manner. How a spirit functions in relation to a body will be an important concept to keep in mind when considering the mystery of the Eucharist.

Now let us reflect on Christ's human nature. By virtue of his triumphant Resurrection, Christ attained "a glorified body: not limited by space and time but able to be present how and when he wills" (CCC 645). Thus, Jesus is able to pass through closed doors (Jn. 20:26) and make sudden appearances at will (Lk. 24:36). St. Paul calls the resurrected body a "spiritual body" (1 Cor. 15:44). Those who are saved will have glorified bodies when they rise at the resurrection of the dead at the end of the world (CCC 999). However, what takes place in the miracle of the Eucharist is something far more profound. First, we must recognize that, given its limited human nature, Christ's body cannot be in more than one place *by the power of that same human nature.* In other words, a limited human body can never be in more than one place by virtue of its own *human* power. In addition, being joined to Christ's divine Person via the Incarnation does not mean that his human nature will thereby automatically partake of his divine power to be present throughout the world. But the Incarnation does make wondrous things possible for Christ's Body, Blood and Soul—namely, the Sacrament of the Eucharist.

So how does Christ become present in the Eucharist around the world and yet remain in heaven? While his body never ceases to be human, let us first consider that Christ enables it to be present after the manner of a spirit in the Eucharist. That is, Christ is present in the Eucharistic elements like our human souls are diffused throughout our bodies: in a whole and undivided manner. Jesus' body remains a body, but, like a spirit, his body becomes miraculously present in a whole and undivided manner in each and every Eucharistic Host, and thus in each and every part of each Host. The *Catechism* (CCC 1377) affirms this mystery:

> The Eucharistic presence of Christ begins at the moment of the consecration and endures as long as the Eucharistic species subsist. Christ is present whole and entire . . . in each of their parts, in such a way that the breaking of the bread does not divide Christ [cf. Council of Trent: DS 1641].[2]

---

[2] In canon 3 of the Council of Trent's "Canons on the Most Holy Sacrament of the Eucharist," the Church provides, "If anyone denies that in the venerable

In addition, while the "substance" or essential matter of bread and wine is transubstantiated[3] into the Body and Blood of Christ, the "accidents" or properties[4] of bread and wine, that is, the color, taste, appearance and feel, miraculously remain (see CCC 1376–77). Normally, if a thing's substance is withdrawn from existence, its properties would

---

sacrament of the Eucharist the whole Christ is contained under each form [that is, bread and wine] and under every part of each form when separated, let him be anathema." As cited in *The Canons and Decrees of the Council of Trent*, trans. Rev. H. J. Schroeder, O.P. (Rockford, IL: TAN Books and Publishers, 1978), 79, footnote omitted.

[3] In his 1965 encyclical on the Eucharist, *Mysterium Fidei* ("The Mystery of Faith"), Pope Paul VI concisely affirms "the dogma of transubstantiation" (no. 10; see no. 24; http://w2.vatican.va/content/paul-vi/en/encyclicals/documents/hf_p-vi_enc_03091965_mysterium.html; see also Pope St. John Paul II's 2003 encyclical *Ecclesia de Eucharistia*, no. 9). "For what now lies beneath the aforementioned species is not what was there before," writes the Pope, "but something completely different; and not just in the estimation of Church belief but in reality, since once the substance or nature of the bread and wine has been changed into the body and blood of Christ, nothing remains of the bread and the wine except for the species—beneath which Christ is present whole and entire in His physical 'reality,' corporeally present, although not in the manner in which bodies are in a place" (Paul VI, *Mysterium Fidei*, no. 46). In saying "not in the manner in which bodies are in a place," the Pope means not in the way bodies are normally present. Rather, as explained above, Christ's Body is present in the Eucharist after the manner of a spirit.

[4] "Accidents" or properties are things that by nature are required to exist in another being or thing. They are also known as "attributes" or "qualities" of someone or something. For example, you never see a "blue." It's always a blue coat or a blue car or something else blue. In the Eucharist, while the substance of wine no longer exists, for example, the various properties of wine continue to exist, including its color, taste and power potentially to intoxicate. For an excellent primer on accidents/properties in light of the Church's teaching on the Eucharist, see Frank J. Sheed's *Theology for Beginners* (Ann Arbor, MI: Servant Books, 1982), 156–58.

naturally perish with it.[5] But the properties of the bread and wine are kept in existence because Jesus gives his body the divine power to coexist with them. That is, Jesus wills his body to go beyond its limited human nature and become a participant in his divine attributes. In addition, Christ's body does not become omnipresent through the Sacrament of the Eucharist, but Christ omnipotently enables his body to have "a share" in his divine omnipresence. Specifically, Jesus enables his body to become sacramentally present wherever the Mass is celebrated and wherever he —our Eucharistic Lord—is reposed in a tabernacle or worshipped in adoration. Fr. Matthias Scheeben helps make the Eucharistic Mystery more accessible:

> Because the body of Christ is the body of the Son of God, it receives through the power of the divine person inhabiting it the unique privilege, similar to the prerogative of the person Himself, but in limited measure, of being present indivisible and undivided in many places and in the innermost recesses of things. Not formally through the hypostatic union, but still because of it and on the basis of it, the Son of God raises the body He has assumed to a share in the simplicity, universality, and pervasive power of His divine existence.[6]

"But," some might protest, "that's humanly impossible!" *Exactly*. For a human person, such a wondrous action is indeed impossible. But when a human body was united to a *divine* Person at the Incarnation, the miracle of the Eucharist became a possibility, for "all things are possible with God" (Mt. 19:26). Again, as Fr. Scheeben notes, Christ's

---

[5] Scheeben, *Mysteries of Christianity*, 474.
[6] Ibid., 476.

body does not automatically (or "formally") partake of his divine powers simply by being united to his divine nature. But the hypostatic union does create the possibility that Jesus can make the Sacrament of the Eucharist a reality, that he can will it into existence. After all, if Jesus can take on a human nature, mysteriously becoming fully human while remaining fully divine, is not providing the Eucharist *also* possible for such an omnipotent God? Fr. Scheeben summarizes the implications and consequences of the Eucharistic miracle for Christ's body:

> [T]he substance of Christ's body exists in a way that is not natural to it, but supernatural to it. We cannot form a direct concept, but only an analogous one of this supernatural mode of existence. For to form a concept of the mode of existence of Christ's body in the Eucharist, we must transfer it to our notions of the natural existence of other substances [namely, created spirits and the uncreated God]. Herein precisely is the miracle and the mystery: in the Eucharist the body of Christ exists supernaturally in a way that only substances of an entirely different kind can exist naturally [again, Fr. Scheeben refers to created spirits and the uncreated God]. Although material in itself, the body of Christ exists after the fashion of a spiritual substance, so far as, like the soul in the body, it is substantially present whole and indivisible in the entire host and in every part of it, and is beyond all sensible perception. Moreover, the existence of the body of Christ in the Eucharist is analogous to the existence of the divine substance. That is, it exists in a way that is naturally impossible even to a created spiritual substance, since it is present not only in a single place, but in numberless separate places . . . wherever the [Eucharistic] bread is consecrated.[7]

---

[7] Ibid., 470–71, 473, emphasis added.

Appendix

The concept is admittedly not a simple one, but Christ helps us understand the Eucharistic miracle through his other miracles, specifically the multiplication of loaves and fish discussed in the first part of John 6. Some Christians who affirm this miracle will nevertheless argue that the crowd ate many *different* loaves. Yet, we must remember that the many loaves that fed thousands had their origin in a *mere five loaves*. That is, Christ temporarily suspended the laws of physics and divinely "stretched" the five loaves to become many loaves, so that the crowd could be fed. If Christ can do that with regular bread, why can't he do something much more extraordinary with his glorified body so that the world can be fed supernaturally? Some may not believe in the Eucharist, but Catholic apologist Karl Keating notes that they should not argue that the omnipotent God is incapable of making the sacrament:

> If Christ, who was on earth in a natural body and now reigns in heaven in a glorified body, can make the world out of nothing, certainly he can make bread and wine into his own Body and Blood. That should not be hard to accept, no matter how hard it might be to fathom. There is no good reason to limit God's acts to the extent of our understanding.[8]

---

[8] Karl Keating, *Catholicism and Fundamentalism: The Attack on "Romanism" by "Bible Christians"* (San Francisco: Ignatius Press, 1988), 243. Keating's argument echoes the Council of Trent, which provides, "For there is no repugnance in this that our Savior sits always at the right hand of the Father in heaven according to the natural mode of existing, and yet is in many other places sacramentally present to us in His own substance by a manner of existence which, though we can scarcely express in words, yet with our understanding illumined by faith we can conceive and ought most firmly to believe is possible to God" (Council of Trent, "Decree Concerning the Most Holy Sacrament of the Eucharist," ch. 1. As cited in *The Canons and Decrees of the Council of Trent*, 73, footnotes omitted).

In his encyclical *Ecclesia de Eucharistia*, Pope St. John Paul II asserts that the Blessed Mother would argue similarly:

> With the same maternal concern which she showed at the wedding feast of Cana, Mary seems to say to us: "Do not waver; trust in the words of my Son. If he was able to change water into wine, he can also turn bread and wine into his body and blood, and through this mystery bestow on believers the living memorial of his passover, thus becoming the 'bread of life.'"[9]

Fr. Scheeben sheds further light on the Eucharistic miracle by means of an analogy. As a single thought can become present to many people through the means of sound waves, so too God himself can be distributed through the means of Eucharistic Hosts at Mass. Here Scheeben cites the work of Guitmund of Aversa, an eleventh-century bishop and theologian:

> We are aware from everyday experience that our thought, that is, the word of our mind, can in a certain way be clothed with sound, so that the thought which was concealed in our mind and was known to us alone can be uttered, and thus manifested to others. Even while it remains wholly in our own mind, it can be wholly made known to a thousand persons through the agency of the sound it has assumed, so that it not only simultaneously illuminates the minds of them all, but at the same time, still whole and entire, strikes the ears of all with the sound in which it is embodied. If, then, God has conferred such power on the human word that not only the word itself, but the sound wherewith it is it clothed, can at the same time reach a thousand people without any cleavage

---

[9] Pope St. John Paul II, *Ecclesia de Eucharistia*, no. 54.

of its being, no one ought to refuse to believe the same, even if he cannot understand it, of the only and omnipotent and co-eternal word of the omnipotent Father, and of the flesh in which He is clothed, so that the Word Himself may be known to us [in the Eucharist]. Neither can we understand the matter as regards the tenuous and fleeting word of a man, and the sounds which scarcely hover in existence for a second, and yet we accept it on the basis of daily experience.[10]

Scheeben wrote in the late nineteenth century, before the invention of radio and television. The analogy he cites becomes even more compelling when we consider the worldwide impact broadcast technology can have on a single, uttered word.

In summary, the body of Christ can be both in heaven and on earth because the omnipotent Christ wills it for our salvific benefit. While Christ's human body is limited in itself, it can share in God's divine power by Christ's willing that it do so.

The Appendix is excerpted with permission from The Biblical Roots of the Mass, Sophia Institute Press. Copyright © 2004, 2015 by Thomas J. Nash

---

[10] Scheeben, *Mysteries of Christianity*, 515–16, emphasis added.

Scripture Index

Genesis

1:26–27, 28, 70
2:23–24, 167
3:7, 182
3:15, 42
4, 112
9:4, 126
12:1–3, 43
12:3, 44
12:4, 43
14, 112
14:17–20, 134
15, 43
15—18, 30
15:6, 43
16, 43
17:5, 43, 53
17:6–7, 43
17:15, 43
17:17, 43
22, 112
22:1–2, 44
22:15–18, 44
32:28, 44, 53

Exodus

2:20–22, 45
3:14, 20
12, 112
12:6–8, 117
12:1–13, 118
12:5, 117
12:46, 117
24, 44, 112
29:40, 134
32, 45
32:29, 45
40:12–15, 45

Leviticus

16, 112, 128
16:1–2, 129
17:10–14, 126

Numbers

3:10, 129
12:1, 45
12:2, 45
12:10, 45
16, 45
16:2, 16–18, 47
16:3, 46
16:28–35, 47
18:7, 129
20, 31

Deuteronomy

4:39, 208
13:1–5, 126
18:10–12, 146
32:42, 125

217

1 Samuel

13:14, 31
28:3–19, 146

2 Samuel

3:4, 151
7:12–19, 43
11—12, 31

1 Kings

1:11–16, 22, 151
2:13–23, 151

2 Kings

13:20–21, 149

2 Chronicles

15:16, 151

Psalms

5:9, 83
10:7, 83
14:3, 83
27:2, 125
27:2–3, 124
36:1, 83
107, 20
140:3, 83

Isaiah

22:15, 48
22:15–17, 19–22, 48
40:31, 155

53, 63
59:7–8, 83

Jeremiah

31:31–34, 49, 127

Ezekiel

36:24–28, 127

Jonah

1:17—3:3, 21

Malachi

1:11, 165

2 Maccabees

12:44–46, 175

Matthew

1:18–25, 141
3:11, 161
3:15, 161
5—7, 79
5:11–12, 188
5:17, 161, 202
5:20, 79
5:35, 208
5:43–48, 177
5:44, 144
5:48, 153
6:9–10, 208
6:12, 166
6:14–15, 79
7:7–12, 156

7:13–14, 79, 80
7:21–23, 80
8, 20
8:28–29, 190
9:2–8, 15, 21
9:37–38, 153
10:3, 63
10:37–39, 155
10:38–39, 175
12, 89
12:1–14, 70
12:33–37, 171
12:35–37, 89
12:37, 89
12:38–40, 21
13:53–58, 140
14, 20
15, 95, 96, 97, 98
15:1–9, 66
15:10–14, 96
15:10–20, 98
15:13, 97
16:16–19, 40
16:18, 32, 37, 52, 53, 54
16:18–19, 22, 176, 183
16:19, 32, 34, 50, 62, 166
16:21, 15, 117
16:24–26, 155, 171
16:24–27, 79, 175
16:27, 171
17:1–8, 146
18:1–4, 183
18:15–18, 34, 54, 176
18:18, 62, 166
18:23–35, 172
18:24, 172
18:34–35, 172

19:4–8, 167
19:9, 167
19:13–15, 81, 183
19:16, 77
19:16–26, 78
19:17, 93
19:26, 211
19:28, 32
21:9, 49
22:31–32, 40, 146
23:12, 46
23:9, 75
24:36, 74
25:31–46, 80, 171
26:26, 107
26:26–29, 117
26:37–44, 183
26:63–68, 21
27:51, 129
28:18, 34
28:18–20, 22, 50, 61, 64, 81,
    119, 155, 157, 183, 191
28:19, 34, 162
28:20, 62, 76, 105, 154, 182

Mark

4, 20
6, 20
6:1–6, 141
8:34–38, 171

Luke

1:30–33, 32, 43
1:31–33, 49
1:38, 183
1:43, 40

2:21–28, 161
4:41, 190
6:26, 188
8:42–48, 149
8, 20
9:1, 190
10:1, 17–20, 190
10:16, 40, 41, 50
14:26–27, 171
15, 147
15:7, 10, 147
22:19, 107
22:19–20, 135, 157,
  182
22:20, 32, 127
22:28–30, 49
22:31–32, 32, 54
22:37, 15
23:34, 98
24:28–35, 158, 182
24:30–31, 65
24:30–35, 164
24:36, 208

6, 20, 118, 122, 124, 125,
  135, 179, 180, 213
6:10, 119
6:26–27, 119
6:30–31, 119
6:32, 35, 120
6:35, 201
6:41–43, 47–69, 121
6:47, 124
6:52, 121
6:52–58, 180
6:53, 121
6:54, 125, 179
6:54, 56, 57 and 58, 121
6:55, 117
6:60, 13, 122, 124
6:60, 66, 179
6:60–64, 123
6:61, 124
6:63, 113, 114, 122
6:63–64, 124
6:64, 123
6:66, 122, 124
6:67, 122
6:68, 179
6:68–69, 181
7:1, 126, 181
8, 21
8:31–32, 57, 204
8:44, 190
8:57–59, 20
8:58, 74, 123, 201
10:10, 15, 175, 201
11:25–26, 5
14:6, 57, 59, 184, 204
14:6–9, 20

John

1:1–3, 14, 74
1:14, 201
1:29, 35–36, 161
1:29, 36, 118
1:42, 52
3:16, 28, 57
3:16–17, 15, 32, 44, 57
3:16–18, 98
3:3–5, 81
5:18, 123

14:27, 204
15:1–5, 144
16:13, 39, 40, 60
17:20–23, 20, 34, 72, 200
19:18, 117
19:27, 151
19:30, 111, 133
19:36, 117
20:21, 33, 61
20:21–23, 158, 166
20:26, 208

Acts of the Apostles

1, 51
1:8, 163
1:15–26, 166
1:20–28, 51
2:1, 161
2:1–4, 5–42, 159
2:14–36, 70
2:37–42, 161
2:38, 81
2:42, 34, 64, 65, 164, 182
5:29, 33–39, 6
6:5, 63
8, 63
8:14–17, 161
8:16, 162
8:26–40, 64
15, 32
16:25–34, 82
16:30, 77
17:16–32, 70
17:24–28, 208
19:1–7, 162

19:11–12, 149
20:7, 11, 65, 164

Romans

2:6–8, 172
2:13, 89, 93
2:13–15, 88, 172
3, 86
3:9, 83
3:10–12, 83
3:10–18, 83
3:28, 86, 89
5:12–18, 42
8:15, 160
8:28, 190
8:38–39, 147
9, 95, 98
9:22, 99
9:22–23, 99
10:1, 99, 145
10:9–10, 103
11:14, 99
12:4–5, 146
12:15, 40

1 Corinthians

1:3, 74
1:12, 52
3:10–15, 173
3:13, 173
4:6, 67
4:15, 75
5:7, 118, 180
6:9–10, 80
7:10–11, 167

11:2, 68
11:23–32, 189
11:23–26, 135
11:27–32, 126
12:12, 146
12:12–26, 40
12:25–26, 147
15:3, 68
15:5, 52
15:42–45, 77
15:44, 208
15:45, 42

2 Corinthians

1:11, 144
5:18, 166
12:8–10, 155, 175, 183

Galatians

1:18, 52
2—3, 86
2:9, 52
2:16, 90
5:16–21, 94

Ephesians

2:14, 112
2:19–20, 54
2:20, 52
4:11–12, 155
4:11–14, 74
5:21, 168
5:21–33, 108
5:24, 168
5:25, 168

5:25–32, 40
6:12, 190

Philippians

1:1, 51
2:10, 190
4:13, 155

Colossians

2:11–15, 81

1 Thessalonians

2:13, 68

2 Thessalonians

2:15, 68
3:6, 68

1 Timothy

2:1, 3–5, 145
2:4, 38, 99
2:5, 139, 144
2:6, 4, 57
3:1, 51
3:15, 40, 64, 76
4:10, 99
5:17, 163
6:15, 49

2 Timothy

1:16–18, 175
2:1–2, 68
3:16–17, 66

Titus

1:5, 163
3:5, 82, 84

Hebrews

4:15, 117
5:1, 134
5:6, 135
5:7–10, 135
7:23–25, 109, 130, 134
7:27, 108, 111, 133
8:1–3, 130
8:1–3, 6–7, 110
8:3, 134
9:4, 129
9:11–12, 118, 130
9:11–12, 22–24, 110
9:11–14, 110
9:11–14, 23–24, 108
9:14, 117
9:24, 130, 134
9:27, 173
9:28, 108, 111, 133
10:1–18, 112
10:14, 112
11:17–19, 44
12:1–2, 148
12:23, 147

James

1:22–25, 88
2, 90
2:14–26, 89
2:19, 190
2:24, 89, 93

5:14, 163, 166
5:14–15, 170
5:16–18, 145
5:19–20, 94

1 Peter

1:6–7, 173
2:5, 163
3:21, 82
5:4, 32

2 Peter

1:4, 77
1:20–21, 70
3:9, 99
3:15–17, 60
3:16–17, 71

1 John

2:1–2, 119
2:2, 99
2:4, 93
2:18–28, 73
2:26–28, 73

Jude

11, 47

Revelation

3:7, 50
5:6, 12, 132
5:6, 133
5:8, 147

6:8, 32

8:3, 147

12:17, 151

17:14, 49, 62

19:9, 137, 180

19:16, 49

20:1–15, 32

21:27, 80, 174, 176

Catechism of the Catholic Church (CCC) Index

CCC no.

74–90, 40
75–76, 58
76, 64, 104
78, 64
84, 59, 74, 104
105–8, 59, 76
156, 24
232–34, 157
253–67, 157
327–30, 142
362–68, 208
374–79, 41
375, 81
391–95, 142, 189
402–6, 41
402–7, 80
405, 81
410–12, 42
413–15, 189
456, 207
460, 77
461–63, 207
464–69, 208
472–74, 75
474, 75
484–86, 208
522, 112
527, 81

536, 161
553, 166, 176
613, 154
645, 208
659–67, 157
662, 112
671–79, 105
673–82, 76
730, 166
731–32, 158
811–12, 142
811–16, 12, 92
815, 34
830ff., 142
838, 38
839–43, 38
846, 38
846–48, 176
847, 38
848, 38
874–77, 136
888–92, 72
890–91, 54, 74, 104
891–92, 72
946–59, 142
999, 208
1030–32, 139, 170
1033–37, 57
1037, 99
1042–50, 57

1067, 154
1076, 81, 158
1085, 154
1113, 153
1114–16, 153
1116, 158
1129, 153
1131, 153
1211, 154
1212, 156, 157
1215, 82
1223, 157
1240, 157
1257, 38
1262, 81
1265–66, 70
1266, 81
1285, 158
1288, 162
1300, 158
1302, 159
1303, 160
1304, 158
1307, 159
1312–14, 158
1313, 162
1322, 159
1323–27, 200
1324, 107, 154, 180
1328–32, 107
1329, 182
1347, 158
1366, 109
1367, 108
1369, 108
1371, 175

1373, 109
1374, 109
1376–77, 109, 210
1377, 117, 209
1378, 109
1378–79, 109
1399, 107, 108
1399–1400, 165
1413, 109
1420ff., 169
1441–42, 167
1443–45, 166
1461ff., 166
1461–67, 166
1471, 176
1471–73, 176
1472, 172, 174, 35
1514–15, 169
1520, 169, 170
1520–21, 169
1522–23, 169
1524–25, 170
1532, 170
1533–35, 163
1534, 167
1546, 163
1547, 164
1554ff., 163
1557, 164
1566, 136
1571, 163
1625–32, 168
1644–45, 168
1804–29, 82
1830–32, 82
1847, 174

1854–64, 80
1855–61, 93
1987, 81
1988, 77
1991, 82
1997–2000, 81
2006–16, 82
2035, 54, 72, 74, 104

2115–17, 146
2284–87, 33
2305, 112
2676–79, 156
2683, 149
2708, 156
2759, 156

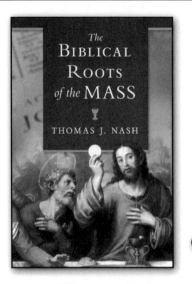